GENESIS

GENESIS

PART II: GOD AND HIS FAMILY
GENESIS 12–50

by Gayle Somers with Sarah Christmyer

EMMAUS ROAD
PUBLISHING

Steubenville, Ohio
A Division of Catholics United for the Faith

Emmaus Road Publishing
827 North Fourth Street
Steubenville, OH 43952

Library of Congress Control Number: 2006924101
ISBN: 1-931018-33-2

Cover design and layout by
Beth Hart

Cover artwork:
Flinck, *Isaac Blessing Jacob*

To my husband, Gary,
whose steady encouragement has been
a light on my path.

—Gayle Somers

To Mark, for his love
and unflagging support.

—Sarah Christmyer

Table of Contents

Hearts Aflame Scripture Study

In the last chapter of Luke's Gospel, we have a wonderful account of a Catholic Bible study. It was the day of the Resurrection, and Luke tells us that two of Jesus' disciples were heading out from Jerusalem to a nearby town called Emmaus. They were "talking with each other" about all the things that had just happened. Mysteriously, "Jesus himself drew near and went with them. But their eyes were kept from recognizing him" (Lk. 24:15–16). He asked them what they were discussing. With a mixture of sadness and confusion, they told Him how their high hopes for Jesus had been dashed with the Crucifixion. They also told Him there was a report by some of the women that the tomb in which He had been buried was empty when they visited it; they hardly knew what to make of that.

Jesus chided them for their foolishness and their denseness. "O foolish men, and slow of heart to believe all that the prophets have spoken!" (Lk. 24:25). The remedy for their malaise was right under their noses, so to speak—in the Scriptures. Starting with the first book of the Old Testament, Jesus interpreted it all for them, showing how all the words, which surely were so familiar to them as Jews, had a much deeper meaning than they realized. He showed them how all of it was about Him, making it clear that everything that had happened to Him, including the Crucifixion, had been foretold.

When the company reached their destination, the two disciples, still unaware of Jesus' identity, begged Him not to go any farther. "Stay with us," they urged Him (Lk. 24:29). Their "Bible study" had deeply affected them; they didn't want to let this man out of their sight.

Jesus went in to stay with them. "When he was at table with them, he took the bread and blessed, and broke it, and gave it to them. And their eyes were opened and they recognized him" (Lk. 24:30–31). He was gone in a flash, but the disciples' dazzling experience with Him on the road, as they listened to Him teach them from Scripture, lingered with them. "Did not our hearts burn within us while he talked to us on the road, while he opened to us the scriptures?" (Lk. 24:32). Energized by this encounter with the resurrected Jesus, they rushed back to Jerusalem "that same hour" to make a report to the apostles about what had happened to them. The eleven had already gotten the good news, because the Lord had appeared to Peter, too. The Emmaus disciples "told what had happened on the road, and how he was known to them in the breaking of the bread" (24:35). A Bible study *and* the Eucharist had fully revealed Jesus to them.

From that day to this, the Church has told us that there are two ways of "knowing" Jesus—through Word and Sacrament. We see this, for example, in the Mass. "The Church has always venerated the divine Scriptures just as she venerates the body of the Lord, since, especially in the sacred liturgy, she unceasingly receives and offers to the faithful the bread of life from the table both of God's word and of Christ's body."[1] The witness of the saints confirms this: "I have a question for you, brothers and sisters. Which do you think more important—the word of God or the body of Christ? If you want to answer correctly, you must tell me that the word of God is not less important than the body of Christ! How careful we are, when the body of Christ is distributed to us, not to let any bit of it fall to the ground from our hand! But we should be just as careful not to let slip from our hearts the word of God."[2]

Although Catholic liturgy and Tradition preserve a proper reverence for Scripture, the "burning hearts" produced by the glorious Bible study on the Emmaus road still eludes many Catholics today. Hearts Aflame Scripture Study aims to help Catholics recover their heritage of lives energized by the illumination, wisdom, and presence of Jesus in His Word. Bible study is a profoundly Catholic thing to do.

Hearts Aflame Scripture Study

Hearts Aflame Scripture Study is built upon the conviction that the Scripture is not a textbook, even though we "study" it; rather, it is a place of encounter with God. "For in the sacred books, the Father who is in heaven meets His children with great love and speaks with them; and the force and power in the word of God is so great that it stands as the support and energy of the Church, the strength of faith for her sons, the food of the soul, the pure and everlasting source of spiritual life" (DV 21). We don't approach the Bible simply to get information. We want to have a genuine experience of entering into the loving conversation that God desires to have with us in His Word. We expect to be as riveted by this as those disciples on the road to Emmaus were. We understand that our recognition of Jesus in the sacraments will be enriched and deepened by encountering Him "on the road," as we read the Scriptures. We are looking beyond information to *transformation*. How will that happen?

Encountering Jesus in the Scripture takes *time*, just as it did for the disciples on the road to Emmaus. Although their hearts were burning as they listened to the Stranger

---

[1] Second Vatican Council, Dogmatic Constitution on Divine Revelation *Dei Verbum* (November 18, 1965), no. 21 (hereafter cited in text as DV).
[2] Saint Caesarius of Arles, Sermon 300.2.

teach them the Scripture, it was only when they extended their visit with Him by inviting Him to stay that He fully revealed Himself to them. This is instructive for us. It helps us to see that patience, curiosity, hospitality, and humility are all important when we seek to know Jesus in His Word. Hearts Aflame Scripture Study is a measured approach to Scripture. It is text-centered, requiring numerous readings of the same passage. It includes opportunities to open our hearts to the fire of God's love, communicated through the supernatural text of the Bible. It encourages lingering over the text, even after a lesson is completed, inviting Jesus to "stay with us" just a little longer. All the elements of Hearts Aflame Scripture Study are designed to help us imitate the Blessed Virgin Mary, who stored up in her heart everything concerning Jesus that she heard and saw and experienced. She pondered the mighty works of God, and so will we.

How to Use This Study

Here is how the material in each lesson is organized: At the beginning of each lesson, there is an introduction that gives just enough background information to get you started—but only enough to whet the appetite. The sooner you get to the passage to read the words and think about them, the more likely those words of Scripture, and not someone else's commentary on those words, will stick like glue in your mind. Hearts Aflame Scripture Study is committed to this text-intensive approach. We understand that this can seem overwhelming for the beginner. In time, however, this method will prove to be worth the effort. Take heart and be patient.

"He Opened to Us the Scriptures" (Lk. 24:32)

After the introduction, you will see the above heading. It reminds us that when we read Scripture, we are seeking a conversation with the Lord in which we expect to hear Him. Before the "study" begins, we simply ask the Lord to speak to us, and then we read through the Scripture passage in the lesson. There may be much we do not understand, but that is not the concern at this point. We are looking for what we *do* understand, and based on that, we will respond very simply to the Lord. This will be a brief, initial connection that we make with Him. It happens through something that is clear to us without any further study. Why do we take the time to do this? It helps us to avoid thinking of Scripture as a text to be mastered. It is a moment of calm response to the One who can speak to us through His Word, even if we are unschooled in the Bible.

How do we make this response? Whatever it is in the passage that clearly catches our eye, we will turn into a simple prayer. Sometimes the response to God's Word can be adoration (i.e., "Lord, I adore You because of what I see about You in verse 47"). Sometimes it can be confession (i.e., "Lord, I myself have been guilty of what I see in verse 23"). Sometimes it can be joy, or a desire to become more like what you observe in the passage (i.e., "O, Lord, please make me as confident in Your power and love as Saint Paul was in verse 18"). Make your response *specific*, repeating in your prayer what impressed you in the passage. There is a place in this section of the lesson for you to write out a simple response to God.

If you get stuck and cannot make a simple response after reading the passage, there is always a "prayer hint" at the very end of this section. It is placed there to make it easier for you to respond to God on your own.

❧

Questions

To assist us in the more rigorous work of studying the passage in the lesson, we have developed questions on the text. Space is provided for your responses.

We used the Revised Standard Version-Catholic Edition Bible to prepare our questions. We recommend it as the best word-for-word translation, particularly helpful for studying Scripture. However, reading the passage again in another version can also be useful. The questions will frequently refer to the *Catechism of the Catholic Church*.[3] You will need to have a copy for your work in this study. To study the Scripture as a Catholic is to share in the experience of the disciples on the road to Emmaus. Jesus interpreted for them the Scriptures—words that were already very familiar to them. And He continues to do that in the teaching of the Church He built. Because of her special charism of apostolic authority, the Church has two thousand years' worth of wisdom about what the Scriptures mean. Her teachings through the ages preserve the interpretive voice of Jesus. She does this by defining dogma, not by giving us a commentary on every verse in the Bible. Dogmas give us the boundaries of belief within which Scripture must be interpreted. The *Catechism* gives us access to dogmatic belief in the accumulated Tradition of the Church; it is impossible to do Catholic Bible study without it.

Some questions are fairly easy; others are not. Some of the more difficult questions are called "challenge questions." If you are unable to respond to those, don't worry. In time, you will find more and more that you are able to have a response to nearly every question. Some of the questions are designed to make you really think. You will need to read the passage over and over. *That's exactly the point!* The more you read those words, the longer they will stay with you. You have your whole life to continue this conversation with God. Do not expect to have responses to every question right away. Be patient with yourself.

---

[3] The Revised Standard Version, Catholic Edition, of the Bible and the *Catechism of the Catholic Church* are available through Emmaus Road Publishing. Call 1(800)398-5470 or visit www.emmausroad.org to order.

❧

Guide to Lesson Questions

In the back of the book, you will find responses to all the questions in the lesson. In order to get the most from Hearts Aflame Scripture Study, refer to these responses only *after* you have answered all the questions yourself. The work you do personally on the text will stay with you longer than anything else in the lesson. Do not short-circuit the process by referring to the responses prematurely.

The responses in the back of the book *are not magisterial.* That is, they are not the "official" Church interpretation of the verses you are studying. They do, however, point you in an orthodox direction. They are designed to enrich your understanding of the texts you study.

❧

"Did Not Our Hearts Burn Within Us?" (Lk. 24:32)

This heading introduces the part of the study that helps us to connect what we've learned with how we live. It helps us to open the door of our souls to the Word of God. For that reason, it is possibly the most important part of the study. It recommends memorization of verses from the text as a wonderful way for God's Word to burn into our hearts. It also asks some questions that are designed for very personal reflection. Be sure to spend some quiet time with these questions. A soul opened to the light of God's Word is a soul transformed.

❧

"Stay with Us" (Lk. 24:29)

This heading reminds us that the disciples on the road to Emmaus wanted to hear *more* from Jesus after the marvelous Bible study He'd given them. They wanted to linger with Him for a while—and this led to His full revelation of Himself. The "Stay with Us" article will always be one more development of the passage you've studied, usually in a slightly new direction. We consider this part to be vital to the Hearts Aflame Scripture Study method; try hard not to think of it as optional. After you have finished the lesson, sit down in a quiet place and ponder again the beauty of God's Word. We believe you will count it worth the effort. Remember that the disciples in Emmaus fully recognized Jesus in the breaking of the bread. You, too, will need to store in your heart what you are learning from Scripture, so that when you are at Mass, you "recognize" Him in the Eucharist. Pondering the lessons is one way for you to keep the truth secure, so that the final step of recognition and transformation can take place. The "Stay with Us" article is there to help you do that.

Lesson Summary

You can use this brief summary as a checklist to make sure that you understood everything in the lesson. We have put it at the very end so it can be an easy reference for you as you start preparation on the next lesson. If some time has lapsed, you might need to be refreshed about what happened in the previous lesson as you work on the new one.

May God richly bless you as you seek Him in His Word!

Introduction

The Book of Genesis

Genesis, with its famous opening line, "In the beginning," and its well-known stories of creation and the early history of mankind, has been often trivialized and isolated from the rest of the Bible by people who don't understand its purpose, or are convinced that modern science has relegated its stories to myth.

That is unfortunate. For the Book of Genesis does not merely tell quaint stories about people who lived at the dawn of time. The roots of all that Christians believe are found here. Read properly, Genesis reveals the essence of the nature of God, of creation, and of man. It shows how man fell from grace and God's friendship. It reveals the nature of sin. In these pages, we see the first hints of God's plan of Redemption and of the promises He made, laying out the blueprint for the rest of salvation history. It is also the beginning of a very important *family* history—that of the family of God.

Genesis is first of five books that form the Pentateuch, otherwise known as the law of Moses. The version we use dates from the time of Israel's return from Babylonian exile, around the fifth century BC. However, Jewish and Christian tradition both attribute authorship of the original draft to Moses, who wrote down what had been preserved through oral tradition or in written fragments around 1500–1400 BC. Its first eleven chapters deal with the origins of the world and mankind; the rest of the book records the action of God in creating the nation of Israel. It ends with the people of Israel living in Egypt, where they sought refuge from famine in their homeland, Canaan. Thus Genesis covers the longest time span of any book in the Bible.

Our study of Genesis is divided into two books: *Genesis, Part I: God and His Creation* covers chapters 1–11, beginning at the beginning of everything and continuing through the history of man, up until the call of the patriarch Abraham, the founding father of Israel. The dramatic story of God's creation of the universe, His design and purpose for everything in it, and His response to the work of an enemy unfolds in those chapters. This is the second book, *Genesis, Part II: God and His Family*, covering chapters 12–50. First, we will examine Genesis 12 to 23 and the rich details of the life of Abraham. We will see how God worked through one human being to restore to Himself the family that was plunged into chaos as a result of disobedience in the Garden of Eden. In chapters 24 to 50, we will follow the history of Abraham's descendants, the very human family through whom God promised to eventually right all that had gone wrong in creation.

Yet it won't simply be biblical history that we learn. Through the historical details, we will encounter the infinitely tender love of God for human creatures. As we observe His relentless initiative to do whatever it takes for men to know and love Him as He originally intended, our study of Genesis will convince us that nothing will impede God's plan for His creation.

In addition, the Catholic Church has recognized that "God, the inspirer of both [Old and New] Testaments, wisely arranged that the New Testament be hidden in the Old and the Old be made manifest in the New" (DV 16). Therefore, our study of Genesis will introduce us to *typology*. "Types" in the Old Testament are real people, places, or events that prefigure in some way the coming of Christ into human history and the Redemption of the world (cf. *Catechism*, no. 128). We will understand Jesus and the Gospel better because of our study of Genesis. We will also see how the Catholic Church has taken seriously every word of truth in this book. By her teaching and her liturgical life, the Church enables us to remain connected to God's original design for His creation. Get ready to be amazed!

Abbreviations

Old Testament

Gen./Genesis
Ex./Exodus
Lev./Leviticus
Num./Numbers
Deut./Deuteronomy
Josh./Joshua
Judg./Judges
Ruth/Ruth
1 Sam./1 Samuel
2 Sam./2 Samuel
1 Kings/1 Kings
2 Kings/2 Kings
1 Chron./1 Chronicles
2 Chron./2 Chronicles
Ezra/Ezra
Neh./Nehemiah
Tob./Tobit
Jud./Judith
Esther/Esther
Job/Job
Ps./Psalms
Prov./Proverbs
Eccles./Ecclesiastes
Song/Song of Solomon
Wis./Wisdom
Sir./Sirach (Ecclesiasticus)
Is./Isaiah
Jer./Jeremiah
Lam./Lamentations
Bar./Baruch
Ezek./Ezekiel
Dan./Daniel
Hos./Hosea
Joel/Joel
Amos/Amos

Obad./Obadiah
Jon./Jonah
Mic./Micah
Nahum/Nahum
Hab./Habakkuk
Zeph./Zephaniah
Hag./Haggai
Zech./Zechariah
Mal./Malachi
1 Mac./1 Maccabees
2 Mac./2 Maccabees

New Testament

Mt./Matthew
Mk./Mark
Lk./Luke
Jn./John
Acts/Acts of the Apostles
Rom./Romans
1 Cor./1 Corinthians
2 Cor./2 Corinthians
Gal./Galatians
Eph./Ephesians
Phil./Philippians
Col./Colossians
1 Thess./1 Thessalonians
2 Thess./2 Thessalonians
1 Tim./1 Timothy
2 Tim./2 Timothy
Tit./Titus
Philem./Philemon
Heb./Hebrews
Jas./James
1 Pet./1 Peter
2 Pet./2 Peter
1 Jn./1 John

2 Jn./2 John
3 Jn./3 John
Jude/Jude
Rev./Revelation (Apocalypse)

Documents

CT   Pope John Paul II, Apostolic Exhortation on Catechesis in Our Time *Catechesi Tradendae* (October 16, 1979).

DV   Second Vatican Council, Dogmatic Constitution on Divine Revelation *Dei Verbum* (November 18, 1965).

FC   Pope John Paul II, Apostolic Exhortation on the Role of the Family in the Modern World *Familiaris Consortio* (November 22, 1981).

FR   Pope John Paul II, Encyclical Letter on the Relationship between Faith and Reason *Fides et Ratio* (September 14, 1998).

NAB   New American Bible. Washington, DC: Confraternity of Christian Doctrine, 1991, 1986, 1970.

NIV   New International Version of the Holy Bible. International Bible Society, 1973, 1978, 1984.

The Call to Abram
(Genesis 12)

Genesis is the book of beginnings; in its first eleven chapters, the beginning of the story of man is told. And it was a bright beginning, because man was created in the image and likeness of God, for His good pleasure and man's own enjoyment. Rebellion against God cast a dark shadow in man's story, however. Adam and Eve were expelled from paradise, under the curse of death. That might have looked like the end, but it was really only another *beginning*.

The story of mankind outside of Eden was the beginning of the account of God's amazing plan to redeem His fallen creation and restore it to its original splendor. It included a cleansing of the sin-stained earth by a great flood, and a new beginning for mankind through the righteousness of one man, Noah. God renewed His covenant with man and set the rainbow in the sky to mark His faithful love for His creation.

In the story of Noah and the flood, however, some ominous clouds gathered in that sky of the newly re-created earth. Noah was a righteous, faithful man, but he was not perfect. He got drunk, and his son, Ham, arrogantly took advantage of his father's weakness. That offense precipitated the pronouncement of a curse by Noah on one of Ham's Sons, Canaan. Suddenly, we are reminded of Eden in ways we hadn't expected. A promising beginning went sour quickly.

As civilization began to develop through the sons of Noah, some of Ham's descendants decided not to spread out to fill the earth, as God had commanded. Instead, they wanted to consolidate their power, building a city called Babel. They even began construction of a tower that reached up to heaven. God was not pleased by this show of arrogance, so He intervened by confusing the one language everyone spoke into many different ones. That made solidarity difficult for men (especially the ones with proud plans for themselves). They had to continue spreading out to inhabit the rest of the earth. One thing became clear, however: the flood did not remove the stain of sin from the earth.

The story of Genesis 1–11 could leave us wondering whether God's plan for mankind fizzled out. Human history up to this point has been decidedly dark. The memory of Eden grows dimmer and dimmer. Is there any hope left? If we are asking this question, then we are ready for Genesis 12–50. In it we will find that God meets every challenge to His plan for man, in ways that go beyond what the imagination might suggest. Because the problem we see in man is man himself, our impulse is to expect that God's solution will work around him or skip over him. Get ready for a surprise. With God's call to a man named Abram, the human story has yet another beginning.

§

"He Opened to Us the Scriptures"

Before we read God's Word, we ought to take a moment to humble ourselves before Him, remembering that His Word is primarily a conversation with us, not a textbook. "Speak, LORD, for thy servant hears" (1 Sam. 3:9) can be the prayer on our lips. Then, read all the way through Genesis 12. Think about what you understand and what you don't understand. Make a simple response to God in terms of what you do understand. Write your prayer in this space:

_____

_____

_____

_____

_____

Now, ask for His help as you work on the questions below.
(Prayer hint: *Lord, thank You for Your unquenchable desire to bless the human creatures You have made. Please bless me today.*)

§

Questions
God Calls Abram

§ **Read Genesis 12:1–3.**

1. The Lord spoke to Abram, a man who lived in Ur, a large city of Mesopotamia, in about 2000 BC. We know very little about him except that he was a Shemite, a member of the family destined to have a covenant relationship with God (because of Noah's blessing in Genesis 9:26–27).

a. What was the first thing God required of Abram?

_____

_____

_____

_____

_____

b. What do you think was the significance of that requirement?

_____

_____

_____

_____

_____

2. *Challenge question*: In just three verses, the word *bless* (or some form of it) appears five times. Think back to Eden (Gen. 1:28) and back to Noah as he got off the ark (Gen. 9:1). What does this profusion of references to blessing suggest to us about what God is set to do?

_____

_____

_____

_____

_____

God's Promise to Abram

The promise that God made to Abram had three parts. First, God would make Abram the father of a great nation. That nation was the nation of Israel, which did not exist before Abram. Second, God would make his "name great," which, in that day, meant not that he would be famous but that he would father a dynasty of kings. Third, God promised that all families on the earth would be able to bless themselves through Abram. This means that through Abram's descendants, God would open a door of blessing for men, reversing the curse pronounced in Eden. During the course of Abram's life, all these promises were transformed into covenants, as we will see in Genesis 15, 17, and 22. How were these covenant promises eventually fulfilled?

- Abram's descendants became a "great nation" (and not just a collection of tribes) at about 1500 BC, when Moses led them out of slavery in Egypt and back to their homeland, Canaan. God established a covenant with Israel at Mount Sinai, giving them a liturgical and civil code by which to live. This distinguished them from all other nations on earth. They agreed to be His people by keeping that covenant.
- Abram's name became "great" in about 1000 BC, when God made David king over Israel. This was a wonderful time in the history of Israel, when their enemies had been defeated, the land had been secured, and David sat on the royal throne in Jerusalem. God made a solemn promise to him that

---

one of his descendants would always sit on that throne. In other words, David began a royal line of kings.

•"All families" could bless themselves through Abram when, in about 4 BC, Jesus, who was a Son of David and thus of Abram, was born. Jesus came to make universal blessing once again possible for humanity. At His baptism in the Jordan, God announced: "This is my beloved Son, with whom I am well pleased" (Mt. 3:17). Jesus established His Church before He left, which would perpetually offer blessing to the world, until His return. Baptism, the initiation into His Church, washes sin away and makes us sharers of the life of Christ. Thus we become beloved children of God, pleasing in His sight, as Adam and Eve once were.

3. See how deeply and completely this promise of universal blessing is rooted in a human being and his descendants. Knowing human history as we do from Genesis, this was a bit risky. Why do you think God chose to work this way?

_____
_____
_____
_____
_____

Abram Sets Out

❧ **Read Genesis 12:4–9.**
   [***Note:*** *Be sure to check your Bible for a map of Abram's travels.*]

4. Read Genesis 11:4 for a description of some of Noah's descendants through his son, Ham. Review Genesis 12:1–4. What was different about Abram, who was Noah's descendant through Shem?

_____
_____
_____
_____
_____

5. Why do you suppose Abram took Lot, his nephew, with him?

_____
_____
_____
_____
_____

6. God appeared to Abram and made a promise to him. Abram responded by building altars, one at Shechem and one near Bethel. He also "called on the name of the LORD," a phrase we first saw associated with Seth, the son of Adam and Eve. What did this suggest about the relationship that was developing between God and Abram?

_____

_____

_____

_____

Abram's Altars

It is worth taking note of the use of altars in Abram's relationship with God. Noah built an altar to the Lord and pleased Him with the sacrifice he made on it (Gen. 8:20–21). Men after Noah everywhere built altars to deities. Through ignorance and perversion, many men worshipped false gods. Yet there was among men a common understanding that an altar is appropriate when men approach the divine. Why? It is because men know instinctively that they owe God something: worship and service (Rom. 1:18–23). The altar represents man's desire to give something to God. In false religion, the offering is made to a deity out of fear or a desire for manipulation. When men worship from the heart, the altar is associated with praise and thanksgiving. In the life of Israel, the altar would take on a central significance in the relationship between God and His people. It would be a visible expression of atonement for sin and of thanksgiving to God. In the life of the Church, the altar continues to be a central, visible expression of the atonement that Christ won for us on Calvary, as well as the place where our offerings of thanks ("eucharist" means "thanks") are joined to His perfect offering as we renew our intention to be His covenant keeping people.

Abram Is Tested

➳ **Read Genesis 12:10–20.**

7. Abram was faced with a famine in the land that he had left everything for.

   a. What do you think this might have done to his faith?

_____

_____

_____

_____

_____

b. What was his response to the crisis?

_____

_____

_____

_____

_____

c. What other way might Abram have responded to the famine?

_____

_____

_____

_____

_____

8. For Abram to tell the Pharaoh that Sarai was his sister was half-true—she was his half-sister.

a. What was the intention of this deception?

_____

_____

_____

_____

_____

b. What was God's response to Abram's weakness?

_____

_____

_____

_____

_____

c. Why do you suppose God didn't just start over with someone more reliable?

_____

_____

_____

_____

9. _Challenge question_: Clearly God intended to build His own nation, beginning with a miraculous birth to Abram and Sarai. Why do you think God picked one nation among all the others on earth to be His own?

_____

_____

_____

_____

🎜

"Did Not Our Hearts Burn Within Us?"

Our hearts will burn with joy when we consciously open them wide to God's Word. Scripture memorization is a good way to get that started. Here is a suggested memory verse:

Now the LORD said to Abram, "Go from your country and your kindred and your father's house to the land that I will show you. And I will make of you a great nation, and I will bless you, and make your name great, so that you will be a blessing. I will bless those who bless you, and him who curses you I will curse; and by you all the families of the earth shall bless themselves.

—Gen. 12:1–3

Continue to welcome Him into your soul by reflecting on these questions:

Abram and Sarai left home and family in order to receive the gift God promised them. They received much more than they lost. The first step to true conversion is a willingness to leave behind whatever prevents us from belonging entirely to God. That can be a situation that is wrong for us, a sinful habit to which we tightly cling, frivolous distractions, etc. Is God calling you to "go out" of anything today so that He can have you for His own?

_____

_____

_____

_____

Have you ever felt like Abram might have when he obeyed God but faced a difficulty because of it? Were you able to accept it as a test of your faith, or did you see it as a sign of failure? Did you learn from it, or did it become a stumbling block in your life? Speak to God about it.

_____

_____

_____

_____

God's plan to restore blessedness on earth was to build a nation. Righteousness is difficult to live alone. Jesus, the descendant of Abram who made all things new, built the Church as a nation of God's people, whose unity will serve to strengthen them in the covenant. How does the Church work that way in your life? How are you working that way for others in the life of the Church?

_____

_____

_____

_____

≋

"Stay with Us"

As we reach Genesis 12, we find that we are about to become deeply acquainted with the lives of two human beings, Abram and Sarai. They are the first people in Scripture who are followed this closely in the narrative. This in itself should serve as a sign to us: "These are important people. Watch them." From the first verse of Genesis, God has been revealing Himself to us in His relationship with His creation. Yet now we will have an extended opportunity to see God at work in very human situations as He moves along His plan to win the world back to Himself.

Abram, whose name will later be changed to Abraham, became the father of Israel. He was the first Jew. In him we ought to be able to see what God intended when He created a nation for Himself. He was, of course, a real human being in real history, but he is also one of God's works of human art. The rest of Scripture, both Old and New Testaments, constantly look back to this great patriarch. If we are attentive, his life will serve as a window into life with God—what it means to be chosen, called, and equipped to live in the blessedness of God. This is knowledge most precious to every baptized believer, since it is what we have committed ourselves to in our baptismal vows. Sarai, whose name was later changed to Sarah, is included in this examination of the life of faith, although her part is not as detailed as that of Abram. Nevertheless, the New Testament says that Sarah, among other things, "by faith . . . received power to conceive, even when she was past the age, since she considered him faithful who had promised" (Heb. 11:11). The miracle that began God's plan took place in Sarah's body. Hers is a life worth watching.

The story of Abram and Sarai will be one that is human and divine. Are you ready for that? It will cause some winces, just as the episode of Abram's lying to Pharaoh created a ripple of disappointment. Yet if we are willing to open our hearts to these human beings, as God did, they will help us to see the gold that God purifies out of vessels of clay like us.

Lesson Summary

✔ God called Abram, a Shemite, to leave his homeland and his father's house for a new country. He promised to bless Abram by making of him a great nation, one with a dynasty of kings, and to extend His blessing to all families on earth through Abram. In this, God promised to resolve the problem that drove Adam and Eve out of Eden. In some way as yet unclear, God would begin a work on earth that would result in man's blessedness. Man would once again be pleasing in God's sight. Details were few, but this promise was a beacon of bright hope for all human beings.

✔ Abram put his trust in God and left home. Turning his back on comfort, safety, familiarity, and perhaps the pleas of his family, he made a clean break with his past to follow the voice of God, whom he did not really know. He went out to receive the astounding gift God offered to him.

✔ Abram grew in reverence of God. He built altars as a sign of this reverence, acknowledging that God is worthy of honor, praise, and sacrifice.

✔ When faced with the crisis of a famine, Abram went down to Egypt with his entourage. When he feared for his life, he urged Sarai to help him deceive those who might kill him because of her. This was not how God wanted Abram to live, so He sent plagues on the Pharaoh's household. God revealed Himself to be with Abram wherever he was, looking after him. Thus Abram entered into a deeper knowledge of the God who had called him.

For responses to Lesson 1 questions, see pp. 131-34.

Abram in the Land of Canaan
(Genesis 13-14)

Although God had once thwarted the plans of men to build a nation for themselves, made memorable by the Tower of Babel in Genesis 11:1–9, the *idea* of human unity producing greatness was not lost. In fact, God showed in His call to Abram that He intended to use human unity, in the form of a nation, to reverse the devastating effects of the Fall from grace of our first parents. This nation was to exist not through the will of men, but through the will of God. By His promises and His power, a human community on earth would be a source of blessing to all families everywhere.

This plan began with a call to Abram, a Shemite, to leave everything and follow God's directions. Abram obeyed, setting off with his wife and nephew. We noted that Abram began to grow in reverence for the Lord, as he journeyed to his destination. We also noted that Abram had much to learn about life with this God. The lessons of faith began in Egypt with a failure of nerve. These lessons continued as Abram returned to the land of Canaan, for he would face many challenges settling into this new place. And although this may seem like a distant story in an obscure land, far removed from matters of importance to us, that is an illusion. By becoming better acquainted with the man Abram, we will have an opportunity to examine closely the character of one who was called to take possession of a gift God wanted him to have—a call just like our own. We will see how God's friends recover when they falter. And in a surprising twist, amidst hard-to-read names of kings and kingdoms, we will meet one of the most mysterious and yet most important figures in the Scripture—Melchizedek, "priest of God Most High."

Stay alert.

"He Opened to Us the Scriptures"

Before we read God's Word, we ought to take a moment to humble ourselves before Him, remembering that His Word is primarily a conversation with us, not a textbook. "Speak, LORD, for thy servant hears" (1 Sam. 3:9) can be the prayer on our lips. Then, read all the way through Genesis 13 and 14. Think about what you understand and what you don't understand in the chapters. Make a simple response to God in terms of what you do understand. Write your prayer in this space:

_____

_____

_____

_____

_____

Now, ask for His help as you work on the questions below.
(Prayer hint: "*Lord, teach me to count on Your help when
trouble comes, just as You taught Abram.*")

§

Questions
Abram Returns to Canaan
§ **Read Genesis 13:1–13.**

1. Abram made his way back to the land of Canaan.

a. What was the first thing that Abram did when he arrived back in the land to which God had called him?

_____

_____

_____

_____

b. What do you think was the significance of that?

_____

_____

_____

_____

2. In Genesis 13:2, Abram is described as "very rich in cattle, in silver, and in gold." Thus he is the first rich man to appear in Scripture.

a. What can we learn about great wealth from this first biblical record of it?

_____

_____

_____

_____

b. What can we tell about Abram's character by the way he settled the dispute over the land?

_____

_____

_____

_____

3. *Challenge question*: What can we tell about Lot from the choice of land he made?

_____

_____

_____

_____

The Lord Renews His Promise
⚡ Read Genesis 13:14–18.

4. God renewed the promise He made to Abram to make a great nation of him. He told him to take a good look at the land itself. He urged Abram to look with his eyes and to walk through it, examining it carefully.

   a. Why do you think this land was so important for Abram to see?

_____

_____

_____

_____

   b. What might have been in Abram's mind as he was looking at it?

_____

_____

_____

_____

5. Abram settled in a place called Hebron.

   a. What was his response to the great promise of God?

_____

_____

_____

_____

   b. *Challenge question*: Read Hebrews 11:1–3, which is a definition of faith. How was Abram's response an example of this kind of faith?

_____

_____

_____

_____

Abram Goes to Battle

❧ **Read Genesis 14:1–16.**

[*Note: This battle appears to have taken place a number of years after Lot had separated from Abram. There were several skirmishes between two alliances of kings—one of five, the other of four. In the course of one battle, the king of Sodom and his people were captured and taken away, including Lot. Abram got word of this situation and went to Lot's rescue.*]

6. Abram showed no hesitation in going to rescue Lot.

a. What does it show about Abram that he was willing to undertake a rescue like that?

_____

_____

_____

_____

b. What other reaction might he have had?

_____

_____

_____

_____

Abram's Victory

❧ **Read Genesis 14:17–24.**

The Blessing of Melchizedek

After Abram had defeated the kings and rescued Lot, he had a meeting with the king of Sodom and "Melchizedek, king of Salem." This person raises a number of questions for us. "Melchizedek" meant "king of righteousness" (see Heb. 7:2); it was more of a title than a name. He could be just another difficult name attached to an obscure place except that the New Testament tells us that Jesus is a high priest "after the order of Melchizedek" (see Heb. 6:20). For this reason, Melchizedek is of great interest to us.

Most modern biblical scholarship sees in Melchizedek a prefiguring of Christ; some scholars suggest that this episode was actually an appearance of the pre-incarnate Christ to Abram. Melchizedek is a mysterious figure. The early tradition of the Church, which continued well up to the time of the Reformation, was influenced by the Jewish rabbinic teaching that he was actually Shem, the firstborn son of Noah who lived a very long time. This is a compelling idea. Shem was the one on whom Noah's blessing had rested. He was destined to be a master over the Canaanites. His priesthood was domestic; that is, he exercised his priestly role as the head of his family. We have seen this in Noah and Abram, both of whom built altars and worshipped God. This priestly role was passed from father to firstborn son.

If Melchizedek was Shem, then what we have here is the great patriarch of Noah's family coming out from the city of Salem (or "peace"; later this place would become Jerusalem) to bless Abram, passing on the blessing he had receive from his father, Noah. He made an offering; it was not an animal, but "bread and wine." He blessed both Abram and God (a priest always mediates between God and man). He received a tithe from Abram, which was a gesture of gratitude and submission. Then he disappeared, not to be mentioned again in the Old Testament except in Psalm 110:4. There David, king of Israel, prophesied (about one thousand years after this episode in Genesis) that the Messiah, Israel's savior, would be a "priest forever after the order of Melchizedek." What did that mean?

Jesus came as Prophet, Priest, and King in Israel. He was of the royal lineage (a descendant of David), but he was not of the priestly lineage. In his day, only those belonging to the tribe of Levi could serve as priests. Jesus was of the tribe of Judah. However, the Levitical priesthood had been instituted at a time of great apostasy by God's people, when they worshipped the golden calf after God had delivered them from bondage in Egypt (Ex. 32:25–29). The first and best priesthood was in the "order of Melchizedek," because it was exercised in a family by a righteous, firstborn son (like Shem). The writer of Hebrews reminds us that Jesus was a priest in that way. He was God's beloved Son, who came in his Father's name with an offering of bread and wine.

7. The king of Sodom made an offer to Abram that had the potential to enrich him with great possessions.

a. Why did Abram turn it down?

_____

_____

_____

_____

b. *Challenge question*: Notice that when the King of Sodom offered him booty, Abram already had a little speech prepared in response to him (Gen. 14:22–23). It appears that Abram had a conversation with God *before* his victory against Lot's captors, in which he had made a promise to God. When do you think this conversation might have taken place, and why?

_____

_____

_____

_____

8. In verse 24, Abram suggested to the king of Sodom that the men who had helped him—Aner, Eshcol, and Mamre—take a share of the spoils. What practical effect would that have had on his relationship with these men?

_____
_____
_____
_____

9. Reflect on all the characteristics of Abram that you have observed in these two chapters. Describe as many as you can.

_____
_____
_____
_____

❧

"Did Not Our Hearts Burn Within Us?"

One of the best ways for God's Word to burn into your heart is to take it deeply into your life through memorization. Here is a suggested memory verse:

And Melchizedek king of Salem brought out bread and wine; he was priest of God Most High. And he blessed him and said, 'Blessed be Abram by God Most High, maker of heaven and earth; and blessed be God Most High, who has delivered your enemies into your hand!' And Abram gave him a tenth of everything.

—Gen. 14:18–20

Continue to welcome Him into your soul with these questions:

Whenever we stumble in our lives with God, the Church offers us the Sacrament of Reconciliation to enable us to "start over," as Abram did. We always have a choice: we can either suppress our sins, or we can admit them and be restored to intimacy with God. Is this a time in your life to return and call on the name of the Lord?

_____
_____
_____
_____

Abram was a man dedicated to his family. In order to keep the peace, he made a generous, unselfish offer. He took the initiative to settle a dispute. In your own family life, is there any place where you could be this kind of peacemaker? Ask God to enable you to seek peace and pursue it. "Blessed are the peacemakers, for they shall be called sons of God" (Mt. 5:9).

_____

_____

_____

_____

When Lot got himself stuck in a nasty predicament, Abram was willing to face great risk in rescuing him. Sometimes we are tempted to let people suffer the consequences of poor choices, especially in our families. Surely this is sometimes the best way for people to learn (that was true even for Adam and Eve). It requires discernment from God to know when to stand by and watch, and when to lay down your life for a rescue (even when there might be the appearance of defending evil). Is there any place in your life now where you need this discernment? Ask Father Abraham to pray for you.

_____

_____

_____

_____

Abram was a man detached from material possessions. His allegiance to God mattered more than being wealthy. Whenever we see this in Scripture, it is good to check ourselves. Is it true of you? Do you tithe a tenth of all you have to God? Do you hold on lightly to your earthly possessions? Have you set your heart on treasures in heaven?

_____

_____

_____

_____

🐝

"Stay with Us"

For most of us, reading the story of Abram and Sarai requires a good deal of effort, due to the fact that they are people of a distant-in-time, foreign culture. We struggle with the names of people and places. We find it hard to really picture the details of their lives. We consider ourselves fortunate if we can follow the story line reasonably well, with the many twists and turns that it takes.

To get to the heart of this story, however, takes something more. It isn't enough to know their lives just as historical characters. This is also a story of intimacy with God, the first of its kind in Scripture. If we learn how to penetrate this story, we will be able to settle into all the rest of what happens between God and men in the drama of Redemption.

In these two chapters, we have to read Abram more by his actions than his words. There is very little given to us explicitly about how he communicated with God. We can tell what he was thinking by how he behaved. The trek he made back to that first altar in Bethel after his return from Egypt was a strong clue. What was he saying to God along the way? What was God saying to him? His act of calling on the name of the Lord at the altar gives us a picture of a human being like us, one who is aware of his own frailty, expressing gratitude to God for His help.

When God drew near to Abram, after Lot separated from him, to urge him to walk through the land and examine it, what was Abram thinking? How did God communicate these instructions? Did Abram hear a voice or see some sort of apparition? Questions like these are inevitable, aren't they? Our only experience of people who have this kind of communication with God comes from what we know from the lives of the saints. Their knowledge of Him and His will doesn't come in a vacuum. We know them to be people of deep prayer, detachment, and heroic virtue. They experience profound (sometimes mystical) intimacy with God in the context of lives given over completely to Him.

Could it have been that way for Abram? The text does not make explicit reference to "prayer" or "contemplation," yet how else would Abram have been able to respond so promptly and valiantly to the king of Sodom's offer of great gain? Previous to his response there must have been an extensive conversation with God in which Abram resolved to do the right thing, fully aware of the dangers that lay ahead as he went off to rescue Lot. Was he praying as he set out? Did he pray as the battle began?

Recall the blessing of Melchizedek on Abram. Plant firmly into your mind's eye this picture of a man of faith—not a perfect man—humbling himself before the priest of God Most High to receive the blessing and to acknowledge his gratitude by giving generously of everything he had. It was a gesture of reverence and of freedom. Abram gives every appearance of a man being drawn deeply into life with God. Prayer must have been a cornerstone of that life. He had come a long way from his father's house, where "other gods" were worshipped (recall Joshua 24:2–4).

Abram still had a long way to go.

Lesson Summary

✔ Abram and his family returned from Egypt and headed for the first altar he had built to the Lord at Bethel. He made a fresh start with God after displeasing him with duplicitous behavior.

✔ To settle a family dispute, Abram unselfishly allowed his nephew, Lot, to select the best land he could see for himself. Unfortunately, the choice he made, based on appearances, included a city of great wickedness, Sodom.

✔ God confirmed His promise of making Abram into a great nation by having him walk through the land of Canaan, taking a good look at it. Although his wife was barren and he had not even a single heir, Abram built an altar to God at Hebron, a gesture of faith, hope, and love.

✔ When Abram's nephew got entangled in a regional feud, Abram went to his rescue. This battle was perhaps an occasion of intense prayer on Abram's part. When it was over and he had rescued Lot, he was met by Melchizedek, priest of God Most High (possibly it was Shem, the venerable firstborn son of Noah). He received God's blessing through Melchizedek, a priest who offered bread and wine. This is the kingly priesthood that would someday belong to Jesus, God's firstborn Son. Abram responded by giving a tithe, the outpouring of a grateful heart.

✔ The king of Sodom offered the spoils of battle to Abram, but he wisely refused, confirming his desire to be only God's man.

✔ In another wise decision, Abram suggested that his allies be rewarded for their participation in the battle, thus strengthening his relationship with them, in case of future need.

✔ Abram was becoming a man of faith and virtue, which was evidence of a growing intimacy with God.

For responses to Lesson 2 questions, see pp. 134-37.

A Test of Faith
(Genesis 15)

As Abram settled into the land of Canaan, he learned lessons of trusting in God and of living virtuously among men. After his falter in Egypt, he made a fresh start, returning to Bethel and calling on God's name. He showed himself to be dedicated to his family, even to the point of risking his life to save his nephew, Lot. He received God's blessing from Melchizedek, king of Salem and priest of God Most High, and he made a generous offer of a tenth of all he owned. In a test of his allegiance, he refused the King of Sodom's offer of great wealth in order to live only in God's debt. He appeared to be a man of solid faith.

From the time Abram left Haran to the time of the events recorded in Genesis 15, probably about ten years had gone by. We will see what effect waiting can have on a man's faith. The promise of descendants and a great nation was wonderful, but it had to begin with at least one heir. Although Abram counted himself as God's man, what was he to make of the time it was taking for the really big event to happen? How would his faith hold up under that kind of test?

In this lesson, we will hear a conversation that Abram had with God about this test. This exchange is the first recorded prayer in Scripture—not, of course, the first time a man had prayed but our first record of a prayer. We already know Abram as a man of faith and obedience; surely he spoke regularly with God. The prayer recorded in Genesis 15 begins the long history of written accounts of what men of faith say to God, especially whey they are tested, and what God answers back. We are all ears.

❧

"He Opened to Us the Scriptures"

Before we read God's Word, we ought to take a moment to humble ourselves before Him, remembering that His Word is primarily a conversation with us, not a textbook.

"Speak, LORD, for thy servant hears" (1 Sam. 3:9) can be the prayer on our lips. Then, read all the way through Genesis 15. Think about what you understand and what you don't understand. Make a simple response to God in terms of what you do understand. Write your prayer in this space:

_____

_____

_____

_____

Now, ask for His help as you work on the questions below.
(Prayer hint: *"Lord, the test of time is difficult;*
please help me always to wait on You.")

🎵

Questions
Abram Questions God

🎵 **Read Genesis 15:1–6.**

1. "After these things" in verse 1 refers to the events in Genesis 14, when Abram rescued Lot, gave a tithe to Melchizedek, and turned down an offer of booty from the king of Sodom. Why do you suppose that "after these things," God appeared in a vision to Abram, encouraging him not to be afraid and speaking about a very great reward?

_____

_____

_____

_____

2. Abram began a conversation with God, the first recorded prayer in Scripture.
   a. What veiled charge did Abram make against God?

_____

_____

_____

_____

b. What indications are there that this was a problem on which Abram had ruminated for a while?

_____

_____

_____

_____

3. God responded to Abram's doubt.

    a. What was the first thing that God did to address Abram's problem (v. 4)?

_____

_____

_____

_____

    b. God took Abram out to look at the stars. What might have been Abram's reaction to this part of God's response to him?

_____

_____

_____

_____

4. Try to picture Abram gazing at the stars. Why do you think looking at the stars helped Abram to put his trust in God?

_____

_____

_____

_____

5. In verse 6, we see that Abram "believed the Lord," and God "reckoned" or "counted" it as righteousness in Abram. In other words, Abram's trust in the promises of God made him righteous. He was pleasing in God's sight. Catholics speak of this as being in a state of grace. This was not the first time Abram had put his trust in God. Why do you suppose this act was especially pleasing to God at this point in his life?

_____

_____

_____

_____

The Example of Abraham in the New Testament

The episode in Genesis 15 of Abram's faith making him righteous is one that is frequently recalled in the New Testament, especially by Saint Paul. For example, in Romans 4:1–3, he writes:

What then shall we say about Abraham, our forefather according to the flesh? For if Abraham was justified by works, he has something to boast about, but not before God. For what does the scripture say? "Abraham believed God, and it was reckoned to him as righteousness." Now to one who works, his wages are not reckoned as a gift but as his due. And to one who does not work but trusts him who justifies the ungodly, his faith is reckoned as righteousness.

At the time of the Protestant Reformation, the question of whether men are justified by faith alone or by faith and good works provoked sharp disagreement. It is worth pausing a moment to consider this. About the passage in Romans, note the following:

- The word "justified" in verse 2 means being in a state of grace, cleansed from sin and pleasing in God's sight.
- Saint Paul's reference to "works" (v. 2) is not a reference to the "good works" that we do out of faith or gratitude to God. The term as he uses it here refers to "the works" or "rules" that made the Jews a nation separate from all others. They included circumcision, dietary and liturgical laws, as well as the Ten Commandments that God gave to Israel through Moses. Many Jews of Saint Paul's day believed that simply by virtue of being born a Jew and observing all the requirements or "works" of the law, they were righteous in God's sight. For them, righteousness was not a matter of faith and trust in God but a matter of keeping all the rules.
- To prove that Jews should not look to their observance of the Jewish law in order to be pleasing in God's sight, Saint Paul uses Abraham as an example. He was, after all, the first Jew. Abraham was "reckoned as righteous" before there were any Jewish rules or "works." In Genesis, circumcision does not appear until Genesis 17. The other "works" of the law don't appear in Scripture until the covenant God made with Moses on Mount Sinai, recorded in the Book of Exodus. In Romans 4:9b–12, Saint Paul writes:

> We say that faith was reckoned to Abraham as righteousness. How then was it reckoned to him? Was it before or after he had been circumcised? It was not after, but before he was circumcised. He received circumcision as a sign or seal of the righteousness that he had by faith while he was uncircumcised. The purpose was to make him the father of all who believe without being circumcised and who thus have righteousness reckoned to them, and likewise the father of the circumcised who are not merely circumcised but also follow the example of the faith which our father Abraham had before he was circumcised.

- Saint Paul's point in all of this is to say that Jews and non-Jews (Gentiles) are all "justified," or put into a state of grace, in the same way—through faith like Abraham's faith and not by keeping a set of rules. It is a gift from God (grace) and not something we earn.

- Notice that Saint Paul does not use the phrase "faith alone" when he writes about Abraham. He simply refers to Abraham's "faith." Saint Paul's use of Abraham as an example of the faith that justifies includes Abraham's belief in God's promises and his obedience that followed from his belief. Saint Paul would never have thought of separating belief from action. Abraham's actions showed that he believed God's promises. The obedience that comes from belief is what Catholics refer to as "good works." They are a necessary expression of faith; faith and good works can never be separated.
- Saint James in his epistle questions whether a man can be saved if he has faith without works (see Jas. 2:14–24). He recognizes the problem that can arise if men speak of salvation by faith "alone"(v. 24). It becomes too easy to forget that faith is actually belief and behavior. Good works are necessary to prove that faith is genuine. That is why Saint James says that it was Abraham's "works" that justified him, when he offered his son, Isaac, on the altar. These are not the "works" that Saint Paul referred to in Romans 4; they are the works that Catholics refer to when they speak of faith and "good works" as being necessary for salvation. This is precisely what Saint James teaches here. He uses Abraham as an example of one whose faith was "active along with his works, and his faith was completed by works, and the scripture was fulfilled which says, 'Abraham believed God, and it was reckoned to him as righteousness'" (vv. 22–23). Catholic teaching avoids the confusion generated by the phrase "faith alone" by retaining Saint James' inclusion of "works" when addressing salvation.

6. The exchange between God and Abram in these verses is an example of prayer. Describe its characteristics.

_____
_____
_____
_____

God's Covenant with Abram

✸ Read Genesis 15:7–21.

7. *Challenge question:* Abram asked a question of the Lord about his possession of the land of Canaan in verse 8. We know that Abram believed God's promises, so this was not a question from doubt. What kind of question was it?

_____
_____
_____
_____

[*Note:* *In ancient Semitic cultures, covenants were sometimes sealed by cutting animals into pieces and having the two parties making the covenant pass between the pieces (see Jer. 34:18). The idea was to demonstrate their commitment to keeping the terms of the covenant by taking an oath: "May what happened to these animals happen to me if I don't keep this covenant."*

In this action, God turned His promise to Abram of a "great nation" (Gen. 12:2) into a covenant with him. This covenant guaranteed land to Abram, because a nation cannot exist without land. The covenant promise was fulfilled when the people of Israel, under Moses' leadership, became God's nation at Mount Sinai and took possession of the land of Canaan as the Promised Land.]

8. Picture Abram setting up this elaborate arrangement of dead animals.
a. Abram had to drive away the birds of prey. What does that tell you about the time factor in this scene?

_____

_____

_____

_____

b. What do you think was going through Abram's head while he waited for something to happen?

_____

_____

_____

_____

9. *Challenge question*: Why do you suppose Abram fell into a deep sleep right at the moment when God came to speak to him?

_____

_____

_____

_____

10. God spoke to Abram while he was asleep. He gave him a somewhat gloomy picture of the future of his descendants. God had promised to make of Abram a "great nation." How do you think years of bondage in slavery could be reconciled with this promise of greatness?

_____

_____

_____

_____

11. *Challenge question*: God appeared as a "smoking fire pot and a flaming torch" as He solemnized the covenant He made with Abram. (This phrase probably indicates only one symbol, "namely, the appearance as of a smoking furnace from which torch-like flames shot out.")[1] Read Exodus 3:2, 13:21, 19:18, and 40:38. Why do you suppose God often appeared as fire in the history of His people, beginning in this scene in Genesis?

_____

_____

_____

_____

♪

"Did Not Our Hearts Burn Within Us?"

One of the best ways for God's Word to burn into your heart is to take it deeply into your life through memorization. Here is a suggested memory verse:

And he brought him outside and said, "Look toward heaven, and number the stars, if you are able to number them." Then he said to him, "So shall your descendants be." And he believed the LORD; and he reckoned it to him as righteousness.

—Gen. 15:5–6

Continue to welcome Him into your soul with these questions:

Have you ever been tested by time in your relationship with God? Are you being tested that way now? Think about how God helped Abram to believe the promises He had made to him, even though much time had gone by. Would you be willing to let Him help you like that, too?

_____

_____

_____

_____

God promised Abram a great nation would come from him, but its greatness would come after a time of humiliation. It is not easy to count on glory when all we feel is smallness, lack of power, and bondage. Think about the places in your life now where you are being humbled. Can you thank God now for the good fruit that will come of it, even before you see it?

_____

_____

_____

_____

---

[1] Francis Davidson, ed., *The New Bible Commentary* (Grand Rapids, MI: Wm. B. Eerdmans, 1960), 90.

Prayers recorded in Scripture are very helpful to us as we grow in intimacy with God. They can instruct us in our own prayer life. Review your response to question 6 in this lesson. Are your prayers like Abram's? Can he teach you something about prayer today?

_____

_____

_____

_____

❦
"Stay with Us"

How interesting it is for us to absorb the details of Genesis 15. One lesson barely does justice to all that it contains. The great example of Abram's prayer, his experience of being counted righteous by faith, and the growing intimacy evident between God and Abram are all topics worth exploring more fully. Yet for Catholics, perhaps the most intriguing element in it is the first evidence in Scripture that God confirms His promises to His people not only in words but also in *liturgical action*. We have seen men build altars and make offerings to God in worship. We have seen God use elements in nature to remind men of His promises to them. Now we see all these coming together in response to Abram's question: "O Lord, how will I *know* . . . ?" The question comes not from doubt, but from faith. It is a human question from a human being. Abram desired the kind of knowledge that is distinctly human—that which comes through the senses. God was ready to accommodate this. In the liturgical action of fire passing between dead animal parts, with God speaking a word of promise, we have confirmation that humans in a covenant with divinity can experience His presence and encouragement in a way they can comprehend. Fire, blood, flesh, and the Word of God, present in this scene in Genesis, all appear again *dramatically* at Mount Sinai, when God made a covenant with His people, Israel, through Moses (see Ex. 24). From that time on, at God's command, they remain central to the worship of God by the Jews, right up to the time of Jesus.

The Incarnation, of course, is the culmination of men's desire to *know* who God is and that He will keep His promises. No wonder, then, that as a priest in the line of Melchizedek, Jesus spoke of bread and wine as His Body and Blood. His words and action combine the elements of the worship of Melchizedek (bread and wine offered in thanksgiving) and the worship of Israel (flesh and blood confirming a covenant). His command to His apostles to do this same action over and over until He returns means that in His Church, men can know in a human way—through a visible, liturgical action of worship—that God will keep His new covenant with them. In this worship, the Fire of God, the Holy Spirit, comes to transform bread and wine on the altar into body and blood. The body and blood will not be that of animals, as it was for Abram. It will be the glorified human presence of Jesus Himself, the Lamb of God who is the Yes to all God's promises. It is then offered as a meal in thanksgiving to God for who He is and for delivering us from death to life.

Catholic worship, therefore, is the *fulfillment* of the worship of the Jews offered when God made a covenant with them, begun here by the very first Jew, Abram, in Genesis 15.

Lesson Summary

✔ God appeared to Abram in a time of doubt. It had been ten years since he left his home, yet no son had been born to him. It was difficult for him to continue to believe that God would keep His promise. In desperation, Abram suggested that his slave would have to be his heir.

✔ God assured Abram that his own son would be his heir. Instead of telling him exactly when that would happen, which might have alleviated Abram's anxieties, God took him out to look at and count the stars, renewing His promise to make many descendants from him.

✔ Abram pondered the night sky, perhaps reviewing all the pros and cons of putting his trust in God. Finally, he made an act of faith. God counted this act as righteousness in Abram. Abram was pleasing in God's sight because of his faith.

✔ The elements of this first recorded biblical prayer included God's initiative and man's response, honesty and intimacy, speaking and listening, silence and action.

✔ The references to Abram in the New Testament, especially in Saint Paul's epistles, use him as an example of one who received the blessing of God ("justification") through faith and not as a result of being a Jew. Saint James warned against misunderstanding salvation as coming through faith *alone*, however. Faith, in the biblical sense, means both belief and behavior.

✔ Abram requested from God a sign of the promise He had made. God directed him to perform a liturgical action, involving animal parts. Abram fell into a deep sleep, indicating that God alone was responsible for this covenant. God told Abram of the future destiny of the nation that would come from him, a future that would involve some suffering before glory.

✔ God then passed between the animal pieces in the form of a flaming torch, renewing the terms of the covenant. This scene is a type of the liturgical action that would become the centerpiece of the true worship of God, both in Israel and in the Church. In it, what began as a promise of God to Abraham to make of him "a great nation"(descendants and land) was turned into a covenant.

For responses to Lesson 3 questions, see pp. 137-41.

The Covenant of Circumcision
(Genesis 16-17)

The passing of years without a son born to him tempted Abram to come up with a new plan to fulfill God's promise. God met Abram in a powerful way during this time of doubt and uncertainty. As Abram was honest about his perception of the dilemma, God heard his honest doubts and enabled him to rise above them. By repeating the truth to Abram ("Your own son shall be your heir") and by directing his attention to the dramatic witness to His power and wisdom given by the night sky, God inspired confidence and trust once again in Abram. His act of faith in the midst of reasons to doubt pleased God, making Abram righteous in His sight.

Yet what about Sarai? How was she holding up during the long time of waiting? This lesson will enable us to see how she responded to her own doubts about God's promises to them. In addition, we will see how God turned a promise into a covenant with Abram and Sarai, when He visited them nearly twenty-five years after they had left home for the land of Canaan. With so much time spent waiting for God to act, what sort of people had they become? What did God expect from them? In their advancing years, will Abram and Sarai have an opportunity for a fresh start and new hope?

※

"He Opened to Us the Scriptures"

Before we read God's Word, we ought to take a moment to humble ourselves before Him, remembering that His Word is primarily a conversation with us, not a textbook. "Speak, LORD, for thy servant hears" (1 Sam. 3:9) can be the prayer on our lips. Then, read all the way through Genesis 16–17. Think about what you understand and what you don't understand. Make a simple response to God in terms of what you do understand. Write your prayer in this space:

_____

_____

_____

_____

_____

Now, ask for His help as you work on the questions below.
(Prayer hint: *"Lord, keep me from ever thinking I can improve upon your plan."*)

❧

Questions
Sarai's Plan

❧ **Read Genesis 16:1–6.**

1. It seems that Sarai had doubts of her own about whether she would ever have a son.
   a. What is the difference between what Abram did, when he doubted (see Gen. 15:2–3), and what Sarai did?

_____

_____

_____

_____

   b. What should Sarai have done with her doubts?

_____

_____

_____

_____

[***Note:*** *It was the custom of the time for a barren wife to give her slave girl to her husband, in the hope of having an heir. "It was not strictly polygamy but rather a means the lawful wife used in order to give her husband children. From what we know of Babylonian laws of the time, if the slave girl became pregnant and then began to look down on her mistress, she could be punished and revert to being treated as a slave."[1]*]

2. Sarai made a proposal to Abram.
   a. What should Abram have done when Sarai made this proposal?

_____

_____

_____

_____

---

[1] University of Navarre, *The Navarre Bible: Pentateuch* (Princeton, NJ: Scepter, 1999), 97–98.

b. What did he actually do (v. 2)?

_____

_____

_____

_____

c. Why do you think he acted that way?

_____

_____

_____

_____

3. What were the unexpected (but perhaps predictable) consequences of this departure from God's plan?

_____

_____

_____

_____

The Birth of Ishmael

✣ **Read Genesis 16:7–16.**

[_**Note:** Because the "angel of the Lord" (v. 7) speaks in the first person as God, most commentators see this as an actual visitation by God Himself and not a visit from a created angelic being. This happens periodically throughout the rest of the Old Testament (Gen. 32:30; Ex. 3:2; Josh. 5:13–15). Some scholars suggest that these angelic visits to men are the pre-incarnate Second Person of the Trinity, the One who, someday, would become the man Jesus. In the Incarnation, Jesus is truly "a God of seeing," as Hagar exclaims in verse 13. The Hebrew there means "a God who can be seen," as is made clear in the last phrase of that verse._]

4. Hagar fled from Sarai's wrath.

a. Why do you suppose that God dealt kindly with Hagar, promising a great number of descendants to her through her son Ishmael (whose name means "God hears")?

_____

_____

_____

_____

b. How did Hagar respond to God's kindness?

_____

_____

_____

_____

37

[**Note:** *Ishmael became the father of the Arab nations, brothers by blood to the Jews yet in constant battle with them, just as God foretold in verse 12.*]

Abram Becomes Abraham

🕊 **Read Genesis 17:1–8.**

5. *Challenge question*: God appeared to Abram thirteen years after the birth of Ishmael. He was ready to turn the promise to make Abram's "name great" into a covenant. Why do you suppose He commanded Abram to "walk before me, and be blameless" as He announced another covenant action?

_____

_____

_____

_____

6. What was Abram's response to this appearance of God and these words (v. 3)?

_____

_____

_____

_____

7. Abram's name was changed to "Abraham," which means "father of a multitude of nations." Why do you suppose his name was changed at this time and not when he first left Haran?

_____

_____

_____

The Covenant of Circumcision

🕊 **Read Genesis 17:9–21.**

[**Note:** *The practice of circumcision was fairly extensive in the world of Abraham's time. The Egyptians circumcised boys at the age of thirteen, which would have been Ishmael's age at this time. For the Egyptians, circumcision was a male rite of passage from childhood to manhood. For the Jews, it was a sign of the covenant God made with Abraham, administered to infants. This is one of many instances when God appropriated an already existing practice and dedicated it to His own purpose.*]

8. *Challenge questions*: The circumcision of grown men, without anesthetic, is painful just to ponder. In addition, Abraham was nearly one hundred years old.

    a. How was this requirement of circumcision really a test of faith, as well as being a sign of the covenant God made with Abraham?

_____

_____

_____

_____

b. Circumcision created a temporary "death" in Abraham's ability to father a child. What significance would this fact have for the menaing of circumcision as a covenant sign to all the descendants of Abraham?

_____

_____

_____

[**Note:** *Sarai's name also changed, to Sarah, which means something like "queen mother" or "princess"—in other words, a name that suggests royalty. From her descendants would come King David, in whom this part of the covenant ("kings of peoples shall come from her") was fulfilled. When David sat on Israel's royal throne (c. 1010–970 BC), God made a covenant with him that someone from his line would always sit on the throne of Israel (see 2 Sam. 7). Jesus, born of the house of David, would be that King, reigning forever over the New Israel, the Church.*]

9. Abraham fell down in a fit of laughter in response to God's promise about the birth of a son to Sarah (v. 17). What do you think his laughter represented?

_____

_____

_____

10. Why do you suppose Abraham begged God to let Ishmael be his heir (v. 18)?

_____

_____

_____

_____

Abraham Obeys God

⚡ Read Genesis 17:22–27.

11. When Abraham heard God say that the birth of Isaac was only one year away, what might have tempted him to delay the ordeal of circumcision instead of carrying it out "that very day" (v. 23)?

_____

_____

_____

_____

[**Note:** *Jews reading the account of this episode would understand the significance of Ishmael being thirteen years old when God appeared to Abraham again. Egyptians circumcised boys at that age, as a rite of passage. Hagar was an Egyptian. Ishmael, later sent away from Abraham's household along with his mother, was not a child of this covenant. Thus, although circumcised, he was not a Jew.*]

Abraham and the Covenant

Abraham readily submitted himself, Ishmael, and all his men to circumcision. As a sign of the covenant, what did circumcision signify to Abraham and to all those who received it that day? Circumcision represented Abraham's formal acceptance of the covenant God made with him. He **believed** that God would keep His magnificent promise of making his name great, with kings coming from him in a royal dynasty. He **agreed** to walk before God and be blameless—to live as God wanted him to live. He **obeyed** God's command to be circumcised, accepting the blood, pain, suffering, and temporary impotence it would cause; he entered into the paradox of "death" leading to life.

This scene is a paradigm of how men enter the New Covenant, mediated by Jesus Christ. We **believe** in the promises of God offered to us through Christ in the Gospel; we **agree** to be God's people through the gift of His grace, walking blamelessly before Him, turning away from sin; we **obey** the call of Christ be baptized, following Him into death that we may follow Him into life.

❦

"Did Not Our Hearts Burn Within Us?"

Our hearts will burn with joy when we consciously open them wide to God's Word. Scripture memorization is a good way to get that started. Here is a suggested memory verse:

> *When Abram was ninety-nine years old the LORD appeared to Abram, and said to him, 'I am God Almighty; walk before me, and be blameless. And I will make my covenant between me and you, and will multiply you exceedingly.*
>
> *—Gen. 17:1–2*

Continue to welcome Him into your soul by reflecting on these questions:

All of us are eager for God's blessing, just as Sarai was. As Christians, we know that God's blessings can seem paradoxical. Read Matt. 5:1–12. Think about whether you are tempted, like Sarai, to short-circuit God's plan for happiness, outlined in the beatitudes, and come up with one of your own.

Read Matthew 4:1–12. Think about whether you are tempted, like Sarai, to short-circuit God's plan for happiness, outlined in the beatitudes, and come up with one of your own.

_____

_____

_____

_____

Abraham promptly obeyed God's command to be circumcised, even though it would be unpleasant. Saint Bernard of Clairvaux wrote: "He who faithfully obeys knows no delay, avoids leaving things for the morrow, does not know what postponement means, gives priority to what is commanded. He is always on the look-out, his ears open, his tongue ready to speak, his hands to work, his feet to be on the move. Everything is done to carry out the wishes of the person in charge."[2]

Are you prompt in obeying God? What tempts you to delay (fear, self-indulgence, sloth, anger)? Speak to God about your desire to act quickly in doing what is good.

_____

_____

_____

_____

"Stay with Us"

Now that we have become well acquainted with Abraham, it is interesting for us to think through some more of Saint Paul's reflections on him, recorded in his letter to the Romans. In Romans 4:16–21, he writes:

[F]or he [Abraham] is the father of us all, as it is written, "I have made you the father of many nations"—in the presence of the God in whom he believed, who gives life to the dead and calls into existence the things that do not exist. In hope he believed against hope, that he should become the father of many nations; as he had been told, "So shall your descendants be." He did not weaken in faith when he considered his own body, which was as good as dead because he was about a hundred years old, or when he considered the barrenness of Sarah's womb. No distrust made him waver concerning the promise of God, but he grew strong in his faith as he gave glory to God, fully convinced that God was able to do what he had promised.

Do you find anything curious about Saint Paul's commentary on the life of Abraham? Would we describe him as a man who "did not weaken in faith"? Would we say, "No distrust made him waver concerning the promise of God?" What does Saint Paul mean? Was he reading the same story we are?

Saint Paul knew all the details of Abraham's life; what he observed of the ups and downs in it must not have counted, in his opinion, as episodes of broken faith. Instead, they must have looked like occasions when Abraham "grew strong" in his faith (v. 20). Saint Paul sees faith as a way of life, not a single act. Faith grows and strengthens; it is tested and purified. It learns from mistakes; it goes forward rather than backwards. In fact, he described his own life of faith that way, in Philippians 3:12–14:

---

[2] Bernard of Clairvaux, *Sermones de diversis*, 41, 7.

Not that I . . . am already perfect; but I press on to make it my own, because Christ Jesus has made me his own. Brethren, I do not consider that I have made it my own; but one thing I do, forgetting what lies behind and straining forward to what lies ahead, I press on toward the goal for the prize of the upward call of God in Christ Jesus.

Although there were surely times in Abraham's life when he could and should have behaved better than he did, he did not pack his bags and go back to Haran. As much as he loved Ishmael, he did not bolt with him to start his own nation. In a true test of faith, Abraham circumcised himself, even though God had said that the birth of his son through Sarah was quite near. At that point, when he willingly disabled the part of his body absolutely necessary for the promise of God to come true, he acted precisely as Saint Paul describes him: "In hope he believed against hope, that he should become the father of many nations" (Rom. 4:18).

The life of faith does not mean a life without failure. Think of Jesus' prediction of Peter's denial: "I have prayed for you that your faith may not fail; and when you have turned again, strengthen your brethren" (Lk. 22:32). Peter certainly failed to do the right thing when he denied knowing Jesus, but his faith did not fail. Jesus anticipated Peter's return and that he would be stronger than ever—strong enough to make others strong.

The life of faith means growth through failure, which is perseverance. Saint Paul saw that in abundance in Abraham, and so have we.

Lesson Summary

✔ Sarai, Abram's wife, had doubts about God keeping His promise of a son, so she came up with her own plan, using her maid Hagar as a surrogate mother. Abram didn't consult God about this idea; he listened to his wife, with disastrous results. The peace of the family was shattered.

✔ Hagar fled from Sarai's harsh treatment; God met her in her affliction, easing her heavy load. She had to return home, but she went back as a different woman—one who had seen God and who had hope for the future.

✔ Ishmael was the son born to Abram through Hagar. When he was thirteen years old, God appeared to Abram to renew the promise of making his "name great" through a dynasty of kings by sealing a covenant with him.

✔ To mark the significance of this occasion, God changed Abram's name to Abraham. This new name began the fulfillment of God's promises to him and his descendants. God was about to build a new nation through His servant, Abraham.

✔ Sarai's name was also changed to Sarah, a name that reflected royalty. She would become the mother of kings. This promise provoked laughter in Abraham, the kind of glee that comes from thinking about two old people being blessed like newlyweds. Abraham showed his deep attachment to Ishmael by making a request on his behalf to God, that he might be the one through whom the promises would come true.

✔ God blessed Ishmael, but He refused Abraham's specific request. The promises would be kept through a miraculous birth. God's plan remained intact.

✔ God commanded Abraham to circumcise all the males in his household. This would be a sign in the bodies of these men and their descendants of the covenant God had made with them. He would be their God, and they would be His people, ones for whom He would do great things and ones from whom He expected obedience.

✔ Abraham's prompt response to God's command to be circumcised, even though it would cause pain and suffering (not to mention the possibility of needing an even more miraculous conception of a child in Sarah), made him an example for all those who enter into a covenant with God. He demonstrated faith in God's promises, acceptance of the terms of the covenant, and sacrificial obedience to the Word of God.

For responses to Lesson 4 questions, see pp. 141-44.

Abraham, Man of the Covenant
(Genesis 18-19)

W e have seen that waiting for God to act can prompt the kind of impatience that leads to imprudence. So it was in the case of Sarah, who urged Abraham to fulfill God's promise of a son by using Hagar, her maid. This was a solution that created lasting difficulties, a pain that could have been avoided had Abraham and Sarah submitted their new plan to God for His approval. Nevertheless, God was merciful to Hagar and to the son born to her, Ishmael. When the boy was thirteen, God appeared to Abraham to formalize into a covenant the promise He had made in Genesis 12:2 to make his name great. He asked Abraham to walk blamelessly before Him, as He repeated the magnificent promise to make him the father of a multitude of nations. God changed Abram's and Sarai's names to indicate that He intended to use them as the foundation for the new thing He was doing on earth—creating an entire nation of people who would be His very own.

The sign of the covenant was circumcision. This act, performed in the flesh of Abraham and his household, demonstrated their unique relationship with Him. Ishmael's circumcision at the age of thirteen identified him as an Egyptian, not a Jew. Although he was Abraham's firstborn son, he would not be the one through whom the covenant promise was kept. Isaac would be that son, born through Sarah. God assured Abraham that the time for that birth was not far off.

Now that Abraham has formally entered a covenant with God, marked in his own body, will there be any changes in their relationship? What does it mean for a man to be drawn up so dramatically in the life of God? What will characterize his life? In this lesson, we will see Abraham at work as God's covenant keeper. These questions we have about Abraham's new role aren't academic. We know that through our faith and baptism, we have also entered into a covenant with God. Who are we becoming?

❧

"He Opened to Us the Scriptures"

Before we read God's Word, we ought to take a moment to humble ourselves before Him, remembering that His Word is primarily a conversation with us, not a textbook. "Speak, LORD, for thy servant hears" (1 Sam. 3:9) can be the prayer on our lips. Then, read all the way through Genesis 18–19. Think about what you understand and what you don't understand. Make a simple response to God in terms of what you do understand. Write your prayer in this space:

_____

_____

_____

_____

_____

Now, ask for His help as you work on the questions below.
(Prayer hint: *"Lord, thank You for Your mercy to the undeserving."*)

❧

Questions
Three Visitors

❧ **Read Genesis 18:1–15.**

[***Note***: *"This new appearance of God to Abraham is somewhat mysterious: the three men stand for God. When Abraham speaks to them, sometimes he addresses them in the singular (as if there were only one person there: cf. v. 3), and sometimes in the plural (as if there were three: cf. v. 4). That is why some Fathers interpreted this appearance as an early announcement of the mystery of the Holy Trinity; others, following Jewish tradition (cf. Heb. 13:2) take these personages to be angels. The sacred text says that one of the three men (Yahweh, apparently) stays with Abraham (cf. v. 22), while the other two, who are referred to as angels, go to Sodom (cf. 19:1)."*[1]]

1. Three men visited Abraham in the heat of the day.

a. How did Abraham respond to the presence of the three visitors?

_____

_____

_____

b. *Challenge question:* Read Matthew 25:31–40 and Hebrews 13:1–2. Why is Abraham's example of hospitality important for covenant-keeping people?

_____

_____

_____

_____

---

[1] University of Navarre, *The Navarre Bible: Pentateuch*, 103–4.

[*Note: Although Abraham possibly did not know at first who these visitors were, when one asked for Sarah by name and renewed the promise God had made to him for the birth of a son within a year, he would have understood that this was a divine visit.*]

2. Look at Sarah's reaction to the news from the visitors (vv. 10–15).
   a. What prompted Sarah to laugh at the idea of having a son within a year?

   _____

   _____

   _____

   _____

   b. Was this laugh like Abraham's laugh in Genesis 17:17?

   _____

   _____

   _____

   _____

Abraham Prays for Deliverance
Read Genesis 18:16–33.
3. The visitors set out and "looked toward Sodom" (v. 16).
   a. Why did the Lord decide to confide His plan to test Sodom to Abraham (vv. 17–19)?

   _____

   _____

   _____

   _____

   b. What did the Lord intend to do by visiting Sodom and Gomorrah?

   _____

   _____

   _____

   _____

4. Look at Abraham's reaction to the Lord's plan (vv. 22–23).
   a. Abraham had a silent reaction to the Lord's plan first. What might he have been thinking during that time of silence?

   _____

   _____

   _____

   _____

b. What was Abraham's concern about the Lord's plan in verse 23?

_____

_____

_____

_____

c. _Challenge question_: Abraham went on to make a request of God in verse 24. He wanted God to spare the whole city if there were fifty righteous men in it. What confidence did Abraham have in God that would have prompted him to make such a request?

_____

_____

_____

_____

The Justice of God

Abraham's concern about the Lord's plan to judge Sodom was that the righteous would perish with the wicked. Thus, their good lives would not be properly rewarded; they would be swallowed up as if they had been evil people. That would be unjust. However, think about the request Abraham made: he wanted the presence of fifty righteous people to "cover" for all the wicked inhabitants of the city. In other words, the wicked would be spared for the sake of the righteous. Is that justice?

If we think of justice as each man getting what is due to him, then to spare the wicked as if they had been righteous was not justice. Yet Abraham believed in God's justice, so why did he make this proposal to God? And, even more amazingly, why did God accept it?

If God were only just, if that were His single and defining attribute, then He would have rejected Abraham's request. Not only did He accept it, but He even allowed Abraham to keep working the number down, down, down. Ultimately, just ten righteous people would save the whole wicked city! Clearly, God was teaching Abraham a profound lesson about "righteousness and justice" (v. 19): righteousness has great power. There is an almost unstoppable, overflowing quality to it. Abraham asked that God allow the "overflow" of goodness in the righteous to fill up what was lacking in the wicked. This would require that God's justice be accompanied by mercy. It asked that out of His sheer kindness, God would accept an arrangement in which His justice against the wicked would be satisfied by "borrowed" goodness.

Why did God go for it? He was teaching Abraham a most crucial covenant lesson preparing not only Abraham's descendants but the whole world for an incredible blessing: the coming of Jesus Christ. One day, the perfect righteousness of one man, God's own Son, would cover the wickedness of every sinner in human history. As Saint Paul writes, "Then, as one man's [Adam's] trespass led to condemnation for all men, so one man's act of righteousness leads to acquittal and life for all men. For as by one man's disobedience many were made sinners, so by one man's obedience many will be made righteous" (Rom. 5:18–19).

Let us never forget that the very first outline of God's plan of salvation for His creation was spoken by human lips, when Father Abraham talked with God.

5. What was Abraham's demeanor throughout this exchange?

_____

_____

_____

_____

Angels Visit Lot

✹ Read Genesis 19:1–14.

[*Note: "The 'street' was an open space within the city, and if a traveler were unsuccessful in finding hospitality, it would be quite the customary thing for him to settle down for the night within the protection of the city walls, but in the open air of this broad square."*[2]]

6. Although Lot probably didn't know the identity of the visitors right away, what did his response to them suggest about the kind of man he was (vv. 1–3)?

_____

_____

_____

_____

[*Note: The sin of the men of Sodom was homosexuality ("know" is the word Scripture uses for sexual intercourse); in fact, we use the term derived from the name of this city to refer to the sex act of homosexuals, which is "sodomy." Cultures given over to homosexuality are ones that are far advanced in rebellion against God and in rejection of His will for men (see Rom. 1:24–27; Catechism, no. 2357–59).*]

---

[2] Davidson, *The New Bible Commentary*, 92.

7. The men of the city surrounded Lot's house. Lot tried to send them away; he also offered his daughters to the crowd to protect his guests. What does this response suggest about the kind of man he was?

_____

_____

_____

_____

8. Look at the reaction of the men at the door to Lot's offer (v. 9). What does this reveal about them?

_____

_____

_____

_____

Sodom and Gomorrah Destroyed
 Read Genesis 19:15–38.
9. Read through the account of the destruction of Sodom and the deliverance of Lot.
  a. What is your opinion of Lot?

_____

_____

_____

_____

  b. Why did the Lord save Lot and his family (v. 29)?

_____

_____

_____

_____

10. _Challenge question_: If we are looking at Abraham's life for examples of how covenant-keeping people live their lives with God, what can we conclude from this lesson?

_____

_____

_____

_____

"Did Not Our Hearts Burn Within Us?"
One of the best ways for God's Word to burn into your heart is to take it deeply into your life through memorization. Here is a suggested memory verse:

So it was that, when God destroyed the cities of the valley, God remembered Abraham, and sent Lot out of the midst of the overthrow, when he overthrew the cities in which Lot dwelt.

—*Gen. 19:29*

Continue to welcome Him into your soul with these questions:

We have seen that hospitality to strangers is a hallmark of a godly life. Do you think of yourself as hospitable to strangers? If not, what small steps can you take to begin building this virtue in your life? Sometimes it can mean a smile at a stranger, letting someone with small, restless children get ahead of you in the grocery line, or using a respectful, pleasant voice on the phone with an intrusive telemarketer. Are you open to being surprised by a divine visit?

_____
_____
_____
_____

Abraham's negotiation on Lot's behalf saved his life. Do you have a "Lot" in your life for whom you must pray with determination? Have you seen anything in this lesson that can give you hope to persevere?

_____
_____
_____
_____

𝄞

"Stay with Us"

Our first exposure to Abraham after his circumcision, when he formally accepted God's covenant with him, is impressive. It was clear that God intended to work with him because he has been called to such an important role—teacher, example, and source of blessing to the whole earth. It is worth taking note of something that might slip by us as we are absorbed in the dramatic story of Abraham's prayer and Lot's deliverance. There was something exquisitely beautiful going on here. And it's only the beginning.

Remember that in Eden, the serpent had a conversation with Eve in which he attacked the character of God. The serpent accused God of being untrustworthy, bad instead of good, and not really caring about the humans. Adam did not defend God's character. There was only silence from him.

In Genesis 18, God initiated a conversation with Abraham that gave the appearance that He was not just. What happened? Abraham vigorously and boldly defended God's character. How? He passionately engaged with God to request that He act in keeping with who He is—the just Creator and Judge of all the earth. What a reversal from Adam's silence in the Garden!

Outside of Eden, beginning with Abraham, God used covenant-keepers to declare the goodness of His character. During the rest of salvation history, it will be human voices that cry out in testimony to the greatness of God and His love for His people. Because of God's covenants with men, never again will there be silence in the face of accusations against His character. After Abraham, it will be Moses, David, and the prophets who extol the majestic perfection of God. In the Incarnation, God Himself took on human flesh to reveal His trustworthiness, goodness, and love. That testimony lives on in the Church, the Body of Christ. Someday all creation, with one voice, will proclaim it: "Great and wonderful are thy deeds, O Lord God the Almighty! Just and true are thy ways, O King of the ages! Who shall not fear and glorify thy name, O Lord? For thou alone art holy. All nations shall come and worship thee, for thy judgments have been revealed" (Rev. 15:3–4).

Lesson Summary

✔ God visited Abraham mysteriously after the covenant had been formalized. He announced that Sarah would soon give birth to a son. She greeted the news with laughter, just as Abraham had done. Sarah, like him, found the news too good to be true. The Lord assured them that nothing would be impossible for Him. Sarah was rebuked for denying that she laughed.

✔ God decided to reveal to Abraham His plan to visit Sodom. He intended to draw him into a deeper knowledge of Himself, making him a coworker. In his role as "chosen," he would be a source of knowledge of "the way of the Lord," a way of righteousness and justice. This Abraham would do by teaching, by example, and by mediation.

✔ God announced His plan to visit Sodom and test it. Abraham knew that He would find great wickedness there, worthy of destruction. He boldly stepped in to suggest that for God to destroy the righteous along with the wicked would give the appearance of injustice and was not in keeping with His character as the just Judge of all. God accepted his proposal to let the righteous spare the wicked, even if only ten were found.

✔ In fact, not even ten righteous people could be found in Sodom. Lot, his wife, and his daughters escaped the destruction, but barely. Lot's wife did not fully realize her deliverance; she looked back at the city and was turned to salt. Lot, who never had learned to master fear in his life, allowed it to drive him into a separated and sad existence. In this deliverance, God proved His justice and His mercy. He had been willing to spare the whole city for ten righteous souls. When He didn't find them, He didn't condemn the righteous to destruction along with the wicked. Because of the prayer of Abraham, which loosed God's mercy, Lot was saved.

✔ Abraham showed himself to be a covenant-keeper. Drawn up into the life of God, he showed hospitality to strangers, trusted in God's character, and, with boldness tempered by humility, interceded for Lot.

For responses to Lesson 5 questions, see pp. 145-48.

A Stumble and a Son
(Genesis 20-21)

Abraham's life as God's covenant-keeper has been a story of growth in faith and in virtue. When three mysterious visitors showed up at his tent, he offered them selfless hospitality. When God revealed His plan to judge Sodom for its wickedness, he urgently interceded on Lot's behalf, obtaining mercy for him and his family. Because of his love of righteousness and justice, Abraham appeared to be a man after God's own heart.

Perhaps at this point in the story, we will want to ask, "Are God's friends perfect?" Abraham seems to have had such an intimate relationship with God that he would not be a man subject to doubts, fears, and missteps. Yet if that were the case, it would be difficult for him to be an example for most of us, since we are often shocked at how fickle and inconstant we can be in our walks with God. And if we are not shocked by our own weaknesses, we are certainly shocked by the weaknesses of others, especially those in positions of authority. In this lesson, we will reflect on a time when Abraham, too, stumbled in his relationship with God.

We will also see the long-awaited birth of Isaac, the son of Abraham and Sarah. The birth of this boy will be the cause of deep joy for his parents, but will also be joy tinged with some pain. The consequences of an earlier lapse will finally have to be faced. How do God's friends behave in circumstances like these?

$$\text{⅔}$$

"He Opened to Us the Scriptures"

Before we read God's Word, we ought to take a moment to humble ourselves before Him, remembering that His Word is primarily a conversation with us, not a textbook. "Speak, LORD, for your servant hears" (1 Sam. 3:9) can be the prayer on our lips. Then, read all the way through Genesis 20–21. Think about what you understand and what you don't understand. Make a simple response to God in terms of what you do understand. Write your prayer in this space.

_____
_____
_____
_____

Now, ask for His help as you work on the questions below.
(Prayer hint: *"Lord, help me not to repeat*
behavior that I know does not please You.")

❧

Questions
Abraham and Abimelech
❧ **Read Genesis 20:1–18.**
[*Note: Abraham and Sarah lived a semi-nomadic existence, moving from place to place. Abraham apparently had a "policy" of claiming Sarah to be his sister, which was half-true (v. 12). Some scholars believe this episode to be a duplication of the one recorded in Genesis 12:10–20, where Abram also disguises Sarai's true identity. While the passages are similar in many details, there is a compelling reason to see these as two distinct occasions: the location in Genesis 20 is Canaan, not Egypt.*]

1. We know that Abraham was deceptive about his true relationship with Sarah out of fear for his life (see Gen. 20:11). He must have known, from his previous experience, that this behavior was wrong. Why do you suppose he resorted to it again?

_____
_____
_____
_____
_____

2. God appeared to Abimelech in a dream to warn him about the situation created by Sarah's presence in his home.
   a. Why do you think God took up this matter first with Abimelech rather than with Abraham?

_____
_____
_____
_____

   b. Was Abimelech entirely innocent?

_____
_____
_____

[*Note: God had apparently struck Abimelech with grave illness, hence He addressed him as a "dead man."*]

3. Abimelech's illness made it impossible for him to have sexual relations with Sarah. Why do you suppose God would go to such lengths to preserve Sarah from being "touched" by Abimelech?

_____

_____

_____

_____

_____

4. God told Abimelech to ask Abraham to pray for his healing, because he was a "prophet" (v. 7). What do you suppose Abimelech's reaction might have been to God's announcement that it would be Abraham's prayer for him that would save him?

_____

_____

_____

_____

_____

Grace through Sinners

Abimelech's healing through the prayer of Abraham is the first example in Scripture of how God does His work through weak and even sinful human beings, if they have been chosen by Him to be in positions of authority, as Abraham clearly had. The work that He does through them is for the sake of others; it does not cancel out their responsibility for their own choices. Another example of this comes later in Scripture, when Moses was in the desert with the rebellious people of Israel. They needed water, so God told Moses to speak to a rock and water would flow from it (see Num. 20:7–13). Instead, Moses hit the rock twice with his rod. In an earlier episode, when the people of Israel had first left Egypt for the Promised Land, God had told Moses to strike a rock with the rod for water (see Ex. 17:1–7). This time, the instructions were different, but Moses didn't obey them. Moses was punished by God for disobeying His word, but God still caused water to gush out from the rock to quench the people's thirst.

In the New Testament, we see the same principle at work. For example, in John 11:45–53, Caiaphas, who was high priest in the year of Jesus' Passion, prophesied that Jesus would die for the nation of Israel. John writes, "He did not say this of his own accord, but being high priest that year he prophesied that Jesus should die for the nation, and not for the nation only, but to gather into one the children of God who are scattered abroad" (v. 51–53). Caiaphas was a man who spoke the most profound truth of the Gospel in his role as high priest, yet he headed up a party of conspirators to kill the Son of God!

In Matthew 23:1–3, Jesus explains how to act towards people who are in positions of God's authority but who do not live up to the truth: do what they tell you to do (because the truth they teach is God's gift to you through these individuals), but don't do what they do. A sinful pope or priest can still be a vessel of God's grace, just as Abraham and Moses and Caiaphas were. Our Catholic confidence in this truth is entirely biblical. (Also see the Catechism, no. 1128.)

The Birth of Isaac
✤ Read Genesis 21:1–7.
5. Sarah once laughed when "three visitors" told Abraham that she would have a son (Gen. 18:9–15). At the birth of Isaac, she laughed again. She lied about the first laugh, trying to cover it up. She expected to share the second laugh with everyone who heard her story. Describe what you think happened in Sarah's heart between those two laughs.

_____

_____

_____

_____

_____

A Problem over Ishmael
✤ Read Genesis 21:8–21.
[*Note: Isaac would have been perhaps two or three years old when he was weaned. At the feast given to celebrate his weaning, Sarah observed Ishmael (who would have been about fifteen or sixteen years old) "playing" with Isaac. Saint Paul, in Galatians 4:28–31, says that this was not innocent child's play but "persecution." The implication is that Ishmael was mocking or taunting Isaac about becoming a "big boy" but not being as important as a firstborn son, as Ishmael was. This was the traditional Jewish understanding of this episode.*]

6. Why do you suppose this kind of "playing" would have so provoked Sarah?

_____

_____

_____

_____

_____

7. Why did Sarah's suggestion displease Abraham?

_____

_____

_____

_____

_____

8. _Challenge question_: Once before, in Genesis 16:1–2, Sarah had an idea involving Hagar that turned out badly. How was this episode, in which Sarah had a suggestion about Hagar, different from that first one?

_____

_____

_____

_____

_____

9. Hagar and Ishmael had to be sent away.
   a. Why do you think God endorsed Sarah's suggestion that Hagar and Ishmael be sent away from Abraham?

_____

_____

_____

_____

   b. Why do you think Abraham sent them off with so few provisions?

_____

_____

_____

_____

[**_Note:_** _On Gen. 21:14, "There is no need to suppose any inconsistency here with the other parts of Genesis, or to imagine this boy of seventeen being carried by his mother like an infant in arms. The privations of the desert reduced both mother and son to exhaustion, but the growing youth would collapse under them sooner than the physique of the mother who had become accustomed to the desert life. Ishmael must have fainted with exhaustion. Hagar did her best to support him, but at last could hold him up no longer and 'cast' him under the shade of a bush."_[1]]

---

[1] Davidson, _The New Bible Commentary_, 93.

c. Although being sent away from Abraham's camp was severe, God tempered that harshness by showing Hagar a miraculous well and by promising to make a great nation of Ishmael. Why was God so kind to the boy and his mother?

_____

_____

_____

_____

A Covenant with Abimelech
𝈀 Read Genesis 21:22–34.
[***Note:*** *This Abimelech appears to be the same one we saw in the previous chapter.*]

10. Abraham had a reputation for being highly favored by God, which would have made him a good ally for the people who lived near him, like Abimelech. Why did Abimelech want Abraham to swear that he would not deal falsely with him?

_____

_____

_____

_____

_____

11. *Challenge question*: See that in verse 33 Abraham called on the name of the Lord. Thinking about what we have seen of him in these two chapters, how would you describe the strengths and weaknesses in Abraham's relationship with God at this time in his life?

_____

_____

_____

_____

_____

𝈀

"Did Not Our Hearts Burn Within Us?"

Our hearts will burn with joy when we consciously open them wide to God's Word. Scripture memorization is a good way to get that started. Here is a suggested memory verse:

> *And Sarah said, "God has made laughter for me; every one who hears will laugh over me."*
>
> —*Gen. 21:6*

Continue to welcome Him into your soul with these questions:

Check your life to see if you are vulnerable to presumption. How can you recognize it? Look for venial sins or imperfections in your character with which you are too patient. Watch to see if you make the excuse of "Well, God doesn't expect me to be perfect" before or after you indulge little selfishnesses. Better to root these weeds out of your life now, before they grow deeper and bind the heart like the chains of a slave.

_____

_____

_____

_____

_____

Has God ever done for you what He did for Sarah—has He ever turned what once seemed too good to be true into a living reality for you? If so, take this opportunity to smile over it once again, and praise Him.

_____

_____

_____

_____

_____

🎜
"Stay with Us"

Think about what we have observed up to this point in Abraham's life concerning prayer. It is really most remarkable. We have seen that God answered his prayers for mercy on Lot's behalf. That was a prayer he prayed out of righteous love of justice and love for his kinsman. We have seen that God showed mercy and favor to Hagar and Ishmael through the intercession of Abraham, even though the unfortunate circumstances that required prayer were due to Abraham's departure from God's plan for him. Now, in these chapters, we have seen God withhold His healing from a gravely ill man until he did what was right (restore Sarah to her husband) and had Abraham, the one who wronged him, pray for him. What can we make of all this?

The best way to understand what Abraham's life shows us about prayer is to remember a thought from the beginning of Genesis. What was it that Adam didn't do in Eden? He didn't pray for help from God. He did not lift his voice to object to the serpent's attack on God's character, and he did not cry out for guidance about what to do next. What would that prayer, had he prayed it, have done? It would have preserved his supernatural grace, the likeness of God that was his as a gift. Instead, he lost it. He was still in God's image, but not in His likeness.

Abraham, as we have seen, prayed. He asked God to act, and the details of his story in Genesis show very clearly that his prayers loosed God's power and mercy. Even when he was weak and culpable, his prayers were efficacious. This is an astounding statement about prayer. As the *Catechism* says, "Prayer restores man to God's likeness and enables him to share in the power of God's love that saves the multitude [cf. Rom. 8:16–21]" (no. 2572). Just as the lack of prayer led to the loss of God's likeness in man, the action of prayer is the first step to its restoration.

When we get to the New Testament, we can hardly fathom the power of the prayers of the New Covenant family of God. What we see here in Genesis of the way in which God used the prayers of Abraham as His instruments for unleashing His power, love, and goodness on fallen human creatures is only a shadow of what lies ahead. If we have been baptized into Christ, we share in that special relationship between the Father and the Son. Therefore Jesus says, "Ask, and it will be given you; seek, and you will find; knock, and it will be opened to you. For every one who asks receives, and he who seeks finds, and to him who knocks it will be opened" (Lk. 11:9–10).

Once it sinks into our minds and hearts that prayer makes us like God and that, because He wants to vanquish His enemy through human beings, He uses our prayers to pour out His blessings on all mankind, we should comprehend why Saint Paul says in 1 Thessalonians 5:17 to "pray without ceasing." Amen!

Lesson Summary

✔ When Abraham and Sarah resumed their wandering in Canaan, Abraham repeated a strategy of deception about his relationship to Sarah that he had used earlier in Egypt. This led to the abduction of Sarah by a man named Abimelech. God caused this man to become gravely ill, so that he could not have sexual relations with Sarah. Then God visited him in a dream, urging him to restore her to Abraham and to have Abraham pray for his healing.

✔ God showed in this episode that His work on behalf of people is not put in jeopardy by the weakness and failure of those through whom He works, if He has placed them in positions of authority. He healed Abimelech through the prayers of Abraham.

✔ Sarah's chastity and reputation were preserved.

✔ In Abraham's old age, Sarah gave birth to a son. She was so delighted with this gift from God that she anticipated the laugh of joy and delight from everyone who hears her story. Her happiness reflected a deepening in her personal experience with God.

✔ When Sarah saw Ishmael "playing" with Isaac, whatever she saw made her realize that sooner or later Ishmael's presence within the family would pose a threat to Abraham's obedience to the covenant God had made with him. She urged Abraham to take the drastic measure of expelling the boy and his mother from the household.

✓ Abraham was directed by God to do what Sarah has said. God promised to show them mercy, but the severe action was necessary in order to break the deep attachment that had developed between the father and his son.

✓ Abraham obeyed, although reluctantly. When Hagar and Ishmael were on the point of exhaustion and desperation, God intervened to preserve their lives and their hope.

✓ Abraham was approached by Abimelech to secure an honorable alliance. The two men formed a covenant that guaranteed them and their posterity peace and well-being.

✓ In evaluating Abraham's relationship with God to this point, we saw strengths and weaknesses. Abraham was obviously God's friend, but we wondered whether that friendship was so secure that little slips (like the dishonesty over Sarah) or inordinate attachments (like the one to Ishmael) just didn't matter anymore.

For responses to Lesson 6 questions, see pp. 148-51.

From Suffering to Glory
(Genesis 22-23)

In some ways the birth of Isaac, the long-awaited son of promise, to Abraham and Sarah seems as if it could be the end of the story we have been tracking through the last ten chapters of Genesis. After many ups and downs, Abraham and Sarah settled into the life that God had called them to so many years before. They never turned their backs on God, packing their bags to return to Haran. There were moments of great faith in their story, and there were also moments of weakness and imprudence. In our previous lesson, we saw in Abraham a strange combination of service to God and man (his prayers for Abimelech's healing) and weakness in his willingness to be less than honest about Sarah. We also observed that Abraham had a lingering fondness for Ishmael, in spite of the word God had given him that his heir would be Isaac. Sarah gave good advice to Abraham, urging him to send the boy and his mother away. It was a severe but necessary move to protect Abraham's fidelity to God's plan for him.

With Ishmael gone and Isaac secure as Abraham's heir, perhaps we could conclude that all the drama of God's plan to bless Abraham, and eventually all mankind, was over. If we are thinking that way, then Genesis 22 will catch us by surprise. Abraham is about to undergo the severest test of his life. What kind of test was it? Why did God put him through it? What are the implications of this test for our lives with God? The drama in Abraham's life is far from over; in some ways, it is only just beginning.

❦

"He Opened to Us the Scriptures"

Before we read God's Word, we ought to take a moment to humble ourselves before Him, remembering that His Word is primarily a conversation with us, not a textbook. "Speak, LORD, for your servant hears" (1 Sam. 3:9) can be the prayer on our lips. Then, read all the way through Genesis 22. Think about what you understand and what you don't understand. Make a simple response to God in terms of what you do understand. Write your prayer in this space:

_____

_____

_____

_____

_____

Now, ask for His help as you work on the questions below.
(Prayer hint: *"Lord, help me to remember that when You test me, You always provide what I need to obey You."*)

Questions
A Shocking Command

Read Genesis 22:1–8.

1. We find in Genesis 22:1 that "God tested Abraham." Why do you suppose God decided to put Abraham to the test? [Hint: Review the response to question 11 in Lesson 6.]

_____

_____

_____

_____

_____

2. Look at the poignancy and the gravity of God's command to Abraham in verse 2. It appears to have come to him in the night, so he had to sleep on it. Describe all the possible reactions you think Abraham could have had to such a command.

_____

_____

_____

_____

_____

3. By early the next morning, no matter what thoughts may have kept him awake all night, Abraham departed for Moriah in obedience to God. How do you think he was able to do it?

_____

_____

_____

_____

_____

4. *Challenge question*: Read Hebrews 11:17–19. When Abraham said to the young men with him that he and Isaac would go worship and "come again to you" (Gen. 22:5), what does it appear he was thinking would happen on Mount Moriah?

_____

_____

_____

_____

_____

5. Imagine the emotions of Abraham as he walked beside Isaac. The tools of sacrifice were in his hand, and his beloved son, under a load of wood, asked him the penetrating question in verse 7. Look at Abraham's answer to that question (v. 8). What was the focus of his mind and heart at that moment?

_____

_____

_____

_____

_____

Salvation through Substitution
🔥 **Read Genesis 22:9–14.**

6. This scene is painfully slow and graphic ("Then Abraham put forth his hand, and took the knife to slay his son"). It's almost as if we are watching it in slow motion. Do you think there is a reason for that?

_____

_____

_____

_____

_____

7. *Challenge question*: When the Lord prevented Abraham from sacrificing Isaac, He gave the reason for such an extreme test. He told him that it was to test his fear of God, whether he would hold back anything from Him. Read your answer to question 1 above. The severity of this test seems disproportionate to Abraham's relatively minor lapses. What do you think explains it? (see also *Catechism*, no. 2572, and 1 Pet. 1:3–9.)

_____

_____

_____

_____

_____

8. *Challenge question*: Picture what Abraham saw when he lifted his eyes from Isaac on the altar: a ram caught by his horns in a thorn bush ("thicket"). It was a sacrificial animal with a "crown" of thorns on its head. Now read John 8:52–59. What might Abraham have seen in that picture that caused him to rejoice, as Jesus said in the Gospel?

_____

_____

_____

_____

_____

"The Lord will provide"

As Abraham and Isaac trekked towards Moriah, Isaac called out to his father and asked about the lamb for the sacrifice. Abraham said simply, "God will provide . . . the lamb for a burnt offering, my son" (v. 8). We have to wonder if that was Abraham's way to avoid telling the boy, "You are the sacrifice." Saying it so directly must have been out of the question. So, Abraham lifted his son's thoughts away from the sacrifice and up to God. In doing that, he became a prophet. How?

When the moment arrived for Abraham to put the knife into Isaac, an angel intervened, revealing the whole episode to be a test of Abraham's faith. At the same moment, Abraham saw the ram in the thicket—the Lord had indeed provided the sacrifice, just as Abraham prophesied. (This was not a lamb, however; that was still to come someday.) Out of the deepest gratitude, perhaps as deep as any human heart has known, Abraham named the place "The Lord will provide." In naming the place, however, Abraham's prophetic work was not finished. It was only the beginning.

That very place, Mount Moriah, later became the place where, much later in the history of Israel, Solomon built the temple, the house of the Lord. The temple, and more specifically, the holy of holies, was where the nation fathered by Abraham worshiped God. Mount Moriah was in a place called Salem in Abraham's day. Later the name was changed to Jerusalem. As Scott Hahn writes,

> Mount Moriah is the place where Solomon (king of Israel in about 950 B.C.) set about building the house of the Lord, the temple that contained the Holy of Holies (see 2 Chron. 3:1). Mount Moriah wasn't out in a remote desert; it was located where the city of Salem was situated in Abraham's day, which later became known as Jerusalem (see Ps. 76:1–3). Why the name change? An old rabbinic tradition attributes it to Abraham, based on what he said after sacrificing the ram: Abraham called the name of that place, "The Lord will provide"; as it is said to

this day, "On the mount of the Lord it shall be provided" (Gen. 22:14). The Hebrew word for "provide" is "jira," which was then prefixed to Salem, thus making Jeru-salem.[1]

Because the place and the form of Israel's worship, built around animal sacrifices for sin, were all given by God to Israel (in great detail, right down to the furniture in the temple chambers and the animal body parts on the altar), Abraham had been right about sacrifices on Mount Moriah—the Lord did provide.

Yet Abraham's prophetic work reached its culmination about two thousand years after he first uttered the words. That was when the beloved Son of God, carrying the wood of the Cross on His back, trekked up Moriah (Calvary is one of the hills of Mount Moriah) to become the Lamb that takes away the sin of the world. The Lord provided the perfect and final sacrifice for sin when Jesus obeyed His Father's will and died in our place. The story of Abraham and Isaac is rich in foreshadows of this event: phrases like "on the third day" and "took the wood . . . and laid it on his son" lead us inexorably to Calvary.

When we understand the truly prophetic nature of Abraham's work on Moriah (recall that God had spoken of Abraham as a "prophet" in Genesis 20:7), it helps us to also understand why God allowed him to go through such a strange and shocking experience. As revealed in the unfolding history of Israel, the prophets of God often acted out His message to His people, in addition to preaching it, to make clear its meaning. So we see that Isaiah walked naked and barefoot to warn Israel to repent; Jeremiah smashed a potter's vessel to show how God would judge the nation; Hosea married a harlot to reveal how Israel had broken her covenant of love with God, her Husband, etc. The bizarre character of this episode puts it as the first in a long line of outrageous behavior to which God called His prophets. All through human history they have dramatized for us the truths about God we need to know, in ways we will never forget. Such was the case with Abraham and Isaac. They dramatized the central event of salvation history, for the Jews and for the whole world.

God Swears an Oath

🔖 **Read Genesis 22:15–24.**

9. Although God put Abraham through a severe test, what was the amazing outcome of his obedience (vv. 15–18)?

---

[1] Scott Hahn, *A Father Who Keeps His Promises* (Ann Arbor, MI: Servant, 1998), 108.

_____
_____
_____
_____
_____

Summary of Genesis 23

In Genesis 23, we discover that Sarah died at the age of 127. Abraham mourned and wept over her, and then he made arrangements to bury her in the land of Canaan (in Hebron). He entered into negotiations with a Hittite named Ephron, and when they reached a satisfactory settlement on a price for "the field with the cave which was in it and all the trees that were in the field, throughout its whole area" (v. 17), Abraham laid Sarah to rest.

---

10. *Challenge question*: If we are wondering what effect Abraham's encounter with God on Mount Moriah had on him, we can perhaps see something of it in Genesis 23. When Abraham approached the Hittites about buying the field in Canaan (the land that would someday belong to his own descendants), he called himself "a stranger and a sojourner among you" (Gen. 23:4).

a. Read Hebrews 11:8–16. What does this passage suggest that Abraham meant when he used those words?

_____
_____
_____
_____

b. What do you think caused Abraham to think this way?

_____
_____
_____
_____

❧

"Did Not Our Hearts Burn Within Us?"

Our hearts will burn with joy when we consciously open them wide to God's Word. Scripture memorization is a good way to get that started. Here is a suggested memory verse:

And Isaac said to his father Abraham, "My father!" And he said, "Here am I, my son."
He said, "Behold, the fire and the wood; but where is the lamb for a burnt offering?"
Abraham said, "God will provide himself the lamb for a burnt offering, my son."
—*Gen. 22:7–8*

Continue to welcome Him into your soul by reflecting on these questions:

Sometimes when we read about God asking Abraham to offer up Isaac, we get fearful of what God might ask of us. We shudder to think of being put through such a frightening test. Has that happened to you during this lesson? If so, speak directly to Him about it now. The tests that come to us from God won't ask us to kill our children, but rather to drive a knife through whatever impedes our growth in holiness. Is there anything you have learned about Abraham's ordeal that will help you to follow his example, who kept his eyes fixed on God and held nothing back?

_____

_____

_____

_____

_____

By the end of his life, Abraham became a man whose eyes were set on his heavenly homeland. He did not expect to find perfect happiness in Canaan or anywhere on earth. This is what we call the theological virtue of hope. Think about how hope liberates us from trying to squeeze perfect happiness out of temporal life—we want our mates, our jobs, our friends and family, the Church to make us perfectly happy. But here's the catch: They can't. Examine your life to see if you have misplaced your hope for happiness. Can you be set free? Can you journey as a sojourner through this world and keep your focus on your true home?

_____

_____

_____

_____

_____

♪
"Stay with Us"

The story of Abraham's life is a story with almost limitless meaning. It includes examples of faith, prayer, and sacrifice. It contains many lessons for those who, like Abraham, live their lives by putting their trust in God. Yet perhaps the greatest significance of the story of Abraham is that it is the story of God in love with man.

From the earliest chapters of Genesis, we have traced out the evidence of God's profound love for the human creatures who bear His image and likeness. The rebellion of Adam and Eve not only did not conquer God's love, it actually became an occasion for Him to demonstrate its depth and breadth and height. Not only did God love humans when they behaved, but He even loved them when they sinned. How? He gave them promises to live by and punishments to purify them. Over and over again, God bent down to reorganize and restore the family life that was shattered in Eden. First, He promised to defeat His enemy through human beings, through a "woman" and "her seed." Then, in Genesis 12, He promised to create, from one man, a whole nation that would belong to Him; and through that nation, He planned to reverse the curse of Eden into universal blessing.

The context for comprehending the significance of Abraham's story is the initiative of God in pursuit of humanity. His call to Abram in Genesis 12 began a detailed, engaging account of how one ordinary human being, a creature of flesh and blood like us, was singled out by God to be transformed from sinner to saint. The story of Abraham's life is the first extended account we have of intimacy between God and man. It is a story of God's love from beginning to end.

Yes, even at the end, when He asked Abraham to give up, to put to death, that which gave his life its meaning, God was acting out of passionate love for him. How can that be? God knows that in losing our lives, we find them. He knew that in Eden. He knew that on Moriah. He knew it on Calvary. The source of perfect human happiness is perfect obedience to God, even if it costs us everything.

The intimations of God's love in the early chapters of Genesis were confirmed and ratified in the story of Abraham. Stooping down to call Abram out of Haran to follow Him to a new country, God demonstrated His condescension to undeserving mankind. Through the details of Abraham's story—faith, missteps, miracles, weakness—we saw how relentless His love is. The culmination of this courtship took place on Moriah, when God rewarded the perfect obedience of Abraham with an oath that would affect the rest of human history, until the end of time. All of God's blessings in the world, from the time of Abraham, can be traced back to this oath. His mercies to Israel, the nation that came from the loins of Abraham, were the result not of the worthiness of Israel but of the promise He had made to Abraham on Moriah (Ps. 51:1–4; Ex. 32:11–14). When Mary sings exultantly of God's work in her, she sees it as a fulfillment of God's promises to Abraham (Lk. 1:54–55).

It is ironic, isn't it, that people sometimes suggest that God in the Old Testament is full of wrath, and only in the New Testament do we see Him as a God of love. Don't believe it for a minute. The story of Abraham is the story of God's powerful love for mortals like us, which searches us out and elevates us to unthinkable heights.

Father Abraham, pray for us to live always in the joy of God's indestructible love.

Lesson Summary

✔ God put Abraham to a severe test, asking him to offer up his son, Isaac, as a sacrifice. Although Abraham had lived faithfully with God for a long time, with relatively few lapses, God wanted to see if Abraham was humble enough to continue to obey Him, even when asked to do the most difficult act imaginable.

✔ Abraham decided to obey God, confident that somehow He would make everything right. He set out with the boy for Moriah.

✔ Isaac questioned Abraham about the lamb for the offering, seeing that they had everything else necessary for a sacrifice. Abraham gave a prophetic answer: "God will provide himself the lamb for a burnt offering." This answer reflected Abraham's trust in God to participate in this act of worship. He did not feel alone and abandoned by God.

✔ At the final moment, the Lord prevented Abraham from sacrificing his son. Satisfied that Abraham's faith was strong and true, He provided a ram stuck in a thorn bush for the burnt offering. Abraham named that place "The Lord will provide." The name itself became prophetic. Abraham could see ahead to a day when God would indeed provide a Lamb for the proper worship of Him by Israel and by the whole world. Later in the history of Israel, it became the site of the temple in Jerusalem. The temple was the place where Israel sacrificed animals to God; the temple was a foreshadowing of Jesus. On Calvary, also on a hill on Moriah, God provided His own Son as the Lamb who takes away the sin of the world, the final and eternal Sacrifice.

✔ God, seeing that Abraham did not withhold anything from Him, swore an oath that He would bless all the families of the earth through Abraham. This oath made the covenant irrevocable. This was the moment in human history when God ratified His plan to restore the human race to Himself, to overcome the rebellion in Eden, to replace the curse with a blessing.

✔ Abraham's act of obedience transformed him into a man who, in his human life, bore the likeness of God Himself. God would one day give up His own Son to ransom the world. Abraham is an example of what obedience to God produces in humans—the glory of the divine nature. As a result of his encounter with God on Moriah, Abraham's heart was set on heaven. He understood that on this earth, he was a stranger and sojourner. Those who set their sights on the "better country" of the city of God become His friends, just like Abraham.

For responses to Lesson 7 Questions, see pp. 151-54.

Isaac and Jacob:
The Blessing Passed Down
(Genesis 24-28)

In the last lesson, we read what is surely the climax of the Book of Genesis. All had been leading up to the moment when Abraham threw himself on God's mercy and did the unthinkable: in obedience to God, he offered on an altar his only son, the very son through whom all God's promises were to be fulfilled. The trial was too painful, and the outcome too glorious, for us to take in all at once. Yet as we watched the drama carefully, we could slowly perceive the magnitude of what happened on Mount Moriah. A son of Adam stood fast on the Word of God; he believed God's promises against all evidence to the contrary. He obeyed to the point of giving up something more important to him than life itself. No wonder James says that Abraham "was called God's friend" (Jas. 2:23). Don't miss the significance of those words. Do you remember what happened as a result of the Fall? Adam and Eve lost God's friendship. In Abraham we see that friendship restored—and that was only the beginning.

God's promise to Abraham unfolded within the history of Israel, in covenants made with Moses and David. It was fulfilled in the New Covenant of Jesus Christ. It takes the rest of Scripture to tell the whole story, but the seeds were planted in God's covenant with Abraham. The time between Abraham and Moses was a time of incubation; the future nation of Israel lay nascent in the chosen family. The remainder of Genesis concerns itself with the development of this family until it was ready, both in size and spirit, to be made into a nation. In order for this to happen, what was a family of three people must grow to enough people to conquer and fill the land of Canaan. It would take several hundred years to get to that point. The leisurely pace of the narrative gives us an opportunity to look at individual lives lived within the context of God's covenant and to see how God molded them even as He made them partners in His plan.

This lesson will cover five chapters of Genesis. Due to its length, parts will be summarized, without any specific questions to answer. In Genesis 24, the focus shifts away from Abraham and rests briefly on the 40-year-old Isaac. Isaac was the original "son of the promise," and he must have been deeply affected by his experience on Mount

Moriah. Although he lived to the age of 180, the real focus of the next ten chapters of Genesis is not on Isaac, but on Jacob, one of his sons. Jacob was the father of twelve sons who became the twelve tribes of Israel, the nation of God's chosen people. His importance in the story is enormous. What kind of a man was Jacob? Watch closely, for the identity of the father would be shared by the nation that came from his loins.

❧

"He Opened to Us the Scriptures"

Before we read God's Word, we ought to take a moment to humble ourselves before Him, remembering that His Word is primarily a conversation with us, not a textbook. "Speak, Lord, for thy servant hears" (1 Sam. 3:9) can be the prayer on our lips. Then, read all the way through Genesis 25:19–34 and 27:1–28:22. Think about what you understand and what you don't understand. Make a simple response to God in terms of what you do understand. Write your prayer in this space:

_____

_____

_____

_____

_____

Now, ask for His help as you work on the questions below.
(Prayer hint: *Lord, help me trust you to keep your promises.*")

❧

Questions

Summary of Genesis 24:1–25:18

When Abraham grew old, he wanted to find a wife for Isaac, the son through whom all the promises of God would be fulfilled. He did not want Isaac to marry any of the "local" women (undoubtedly because of the idolatry practiced by the Canaanites). Instead, he sent his servant back to his own family, to Haran, to find a wife among his kinsmen. God rewarded Abraham's wisdom in this decision by guiding his servant to just the right woman—Rebekah. She was a beautiful, hospitable woman, who was also Abraham's relative. She agreed to leave her family and home in order to be Isaac's wife. Her father gave his blessing to the arrangement, and she returned to the land of Canaan with Abraham's servant.

It was the perfect match. In Genesis 24:63–67, we read: "And Isaac went out to meditate in the field in the evening; and he lifted up his eyes and looked, and behold, there were camels coming. And Rebekah lifted up her eyes, and when she saw Isaac, she alighted from the camel, and said to the servant, 'Who is the man yonder, walking in the field to meet us?' The servant said, 'It is my master.' So she took her veil and covered herself. And the servant told Isaac all the things that he had done. Then Isaac brought her into the tent, and took Rebekah, and she became his wife; and he loved her. So Isaac was comforted after his mother's death."

After Sarah's death, Abraham married again and had other children, through his second wife, Keturah. All of his descendants, through both Keturah and Hagar, were given gifts before he died. He was good and generous to them all, but Isaac was the child of the covenant, the "child of promise" (see Rom. 9:6–8). He was Abraham's sole heir. Abraham breathed his last at the age of 175. His story now becomes Isaac's story.

Jacob and Esau

⚜ Read Genesis 25:19–34.

1. In Genesis 25 we see that Rebekah remained barren for twenty years after her marriage. Isaac's love, however, did not wane. Rather, he prayed to God on her behalf and his prayers were answered.

a. How did Rebekah respond to the fact that her sons were struggling, even before birth, in her womb?

_____

_____

_____

_____

b. What did she learn?

_____

_____

_____

_____

c. What does the way Jacob was born (and consequently the meaning of his name) suggest about the type of man he would be?

_____

_____

_____

_____

2. The circumstances surrounding their birth and their names speak volumes about the two boys and prepare us for what happened next. Ancient laws directed that the birthright—which included the right to at least a double portion of the father's inheritance, as well as the position of superiority and leadership over any siblings after the father's death—belonged to the firstborn son.

a. Why do you think Esau attached so little value to his birthright?

_____

_____

_____

_____

b. Contrast Esau's priorities with Jacob's.

_____

_____

_____

_____

3. *Challenge question*: Read Romans 9:10–16. According to Saint Paul, God chose Jacob (also called Israel) over Esau to father His people. What did God's selection of the younger brother show? Read *Catechism* no. 218.

_____

_____

_____

_____

_____

[**Note:** *In Romans 9:13, Saint Paul quotes the prophet Malachi: "Jacob I loved, but Esau I hated" (Mal. 1:2–3). The Navarre Bible: Romans and Galatians tells us, "The expression 'I have hated Esau' must be interpreted in the light of the constant teaching of Sacred Scripture: God loves everything that exists and does not hate anyone or anything he has made (cf. Wis. 11:24). Therefore, God also loves Esau; but if we compare this love to his very special love for Jacob, the former looks like hatred. This is a very common Semitic way of speaking; our Lord uses it sometimes—for example, when he compares the love he is owed with the love one owes one's parents (cf. Mt. 10:37 and Lk. 14:26)."*[1]]

Summary of Genesis 26

Genesis 26 records a number of events from Isaac's life, events that closely paralleled events in the life of Abraham: there was another famine, as there had been in Abraham's day; Isaac pretended that Rebekah was his sister to avoid trouble with the Philistines, just as Abraham had done with his own wife; God appeared to him, and he built an altar. Although these events were not new, through them God made it clear to Isaac that whatever the obstacles, he was to trust Him and remain in the land, just as his father had done.

---

[1] University of Navarre, *The Navarre Bible: Romans and Galatians* (Dublin: Four Courts Press, 1981), 125.

When Isaac obeyed, God's blessing soon became evident: in spite of the famine, Isaac planted crops and reaped a hundredfold. In spite of opposition from the Philistines, Isaac grew wealthy and flourished in the land God promised him. When he was afraid, Isaac was encouraged by God, who swore to be with him and bless him. Finally, even the Philistines recognized God's blessing: when Abimelech forged a treaty with Isaac, he told him, "You are now the blessed of the Lord" (v. 29).

We can see from Isaac's story that obedience to God's commands was not something God expected of Abraham alone. It was a condition of staying within the covenant relationship. Isaac remained in that covenant, so God's promises and blessing continued through him.

We also discover in Genesis 26 that when it was time for Esau to marry, he chose two Hittite women in the land of Canaan rather than send back to Haran for a wife from Abraham's people. This was a source of great bitterness for Isaac and Rebekah. As we have seen before in Esau's life, the desire of the moment took precedence over heritage and family custom.

Rebekah's Plot

❧ **Read Genesis 27:1–17.**

[*Note: The word for "birthright" in Hebrew is bekorah; "blessing" is berakah. Throughout this account, the sacred author plays the two words and ideas against each other. They both involve the inheritance of the "firstborn," which was a position or title and not just a word denoting birth order. The firstborn became head of the family on his father's death, and as such was both leader and spiritual head of the tribe. He received a double portion of his father's inheritance (cf. Deut. 21:17) along with a blessing: in this case, leadership, prosperity, and—the ultimate blessing—God's promises originally given to Abraham.*]

4. As Isaac grew old and approached death, he wanted to give his blessing to Esau, his firstborn. He asked for a meal from Esau's expert hunting. Esau went out to obey his father's wishes.

a. Why do you think Rebekah pushed Jacob to deceive Isaac and get the blessing?

_____

_____

_____

_____

b. Do you think she was justified in what she did?

_____

_____

_____

_____

Isaac's Blessing

However hard Esau might have cried and pleaded, his father's blessing could not be revoked. It was legally binding and would be effective even under such mitigating circumstances. In the ancient world, blessings (and curses as well) had even more power than we give our legal documents: it was believed that the words themselves, spoken under God's authority, actually accomplished what they pronounced.

Jacob Steals Isaac's Blessing

✦ Read Genesis 27:18–40.

5. Jacob craftily deceived his father, dodging questions and smoothing over Isaac's doubts about his identity. He succeeded in receiving Isaac's blessing.

a. Look at Esau's reaction to the discovery of the deception in verses 34, 36, and 38. What seemed to be uppermost in his mind?

_____

_____

_____

_____

b. Look at what Esau said about Jacob in verse 36. In his anger, how was he also deceptive to his father?

_____

_____

_____

_____

c. *Challenge question*: Esau shed lots of tears in this episode. What kind of tears were they? Also see Hebrews 12:15–17.

_____

_____

_____

_____

"Why Should I Be Bereft of You Both in One Day?"

✦ Read Genesis 27:41–28:9.

6. Rebekah's plot caused Esau to have murderous hatred for Jacob (v. 41). This drove her to form another plot, to send Jacob back to Haran until time passed and Esau forgot his anger.

a. How did Rebekah manage to get Jacob sent away from Esau's wrath and back to Haran (27:46–28:5)?

_____

_____

_____

_____

b. Esau observed Jacob's departure carefully. What did it inspire him to do (vv. 6–9)?

_____

_____

_____

_____

Jacob Flees

⚡ Read Genesis 28:10–22.

7. Jacob set out for Haran, but he spent the first night still in Canaan. While he was asleep, he had a dream.

a. This was the very first personal encounter that Jacob had with God. Everything he had known about God up to this point had come through what his parents had taught him. What did God reveal about Himself to Jacob in this dream?

_____

_____

_____

_____

Jacob's Ladder

In his dream, Jacob saw a ladder extending from heaven to earth, with angels ascending and descending on it. When he awoke, he seemed to believe that the ladder's connection to the ground upon which he lay, the land of Canaan, was very important. He saw it as a place of God's dwelling ("Surely the Lord is in this place and I did not know it!"), the "house of God" and "the gate of heaven." He took steps to hallow that ground, building a pillar there, pouring oil on it, and calling it "Beth-el" or "house of God."

Hundreds of years later, Jesus told His disciples, "You will see heaven opened, and the angels of God ascending and descending upon the Son of man" (Jn. 1:51). He used this figure from Jacob's dream, so well-known to the Jews, to confirm that He was "the ladder" seen by Jacob, in whose Body heaven and earth would truly be joined.

No wonder Jacob awoke from his dream in wonder and awe.

b. Look at the vow Jacob made to God because of his dream (vv. 20–22). What difference had the dream made in Jacob's relationship with God?

_____

_____

_____

_____

✣

"Did Not Our Hearts Burn Within Us?"

Our hearts will burn with joy when we consciously open them wide to God's Word. Scripture memorization is a good way to get that started. Here is a suggested memory verse:

> *Behold, I am with you and will keep you wherever you go, and will bring you back to this land; for I will not leave you until I have done that of which I have spoken to you.*
> *—Gen. 28:15*

Continue to welcome Him into your soul by reflecting on these questions:

It is inconceivable to us that Esau would sell his birthright—the rights to his inheritance and position within the family—for a single meal. But Saint Paul warned Christians (Heb. 12:15–16) not to be godless like Esau and trade away their birthright (they apparently were tempted to compromise their faith to avoid persecution). They needed to persevere in holiness.

Have you ever been tempted to throw away your status as God's child for some physical need or desire, or to deny your faith out of fear of what others will think? How can the example of Esau help you to take your mind off the temporal, and set it firmly on the eternal?

_____

_____

_____

_____

When Esau realized Jacob had cheated him out of Isaac's blessing, he fell into victimhood. He felt so sorry for himself that he "forgot" that losing his birthright had been his own choice.

Are you susceptible to thinking of yourself as a victim, justifying your bad choices as someone else's fault? Love for his father would have helped Esau be more honest. Can love for your Father help you, too?

_____

_____

_____

_____

Jacob was a grown man before he had a personal encounter with his parents' God. That encounter made him vow to love God personally. Sometimes it happens among cradle Catholics that they grow to adulthood without having a personal encounter with God. Are you living off your parents' (or spouse's or friends') faith? If so, can you ask God to meet you personally, as He did with Jacob? Will you be ready for a change when He does?

※

"Stay with Us"

The life of Isaac seems insignificant next to the careers of his father Abraham and his son Jacob. There are few chapters of Scripture devoted to Isaac, and most of his story is entwined with the story of the other patriarchs. Even the *Catechism* moves from "God chooses Abraham" (nos. 59–61) to "God forms his people Israel" (nos. 62–64) without mentioning Isaac by name. Yet he is a patriarch, his name forever included when Israelites call on the name of God, the father of Abraham, Isaac, and Jacob.

Isaac's main role seems to be one of a bridge between Abraham, father of those who believe, and Jacob, father of Israel. Isaac safeguards and transmits the promise through his own faithful obedience. He embodies the continuity of God's promise, the link through whom it passes from generation to generation. But there is more significance to him than that:

- Isaac waits for God's promise, as indeed do all of the patriarchs. Those twenty years spent praying for a son not only helped form Isaac in faith, they became an example for Israel as it waited for God's promised Messiah. As is pointed out in *Dei Verbum*, "through the patriarchs . . . [God] taught this nation to acknowledge Himself as the one living and true God, . . . and to wait for the Savior promised by Him. In this manner He prepared the way for the gospel down through the centuries" (no. 3).
- Isaac is also the fruit, the evidence of God's promise. He is the impossible child, born of two people well past the age of childbearing. His name means "laughter," and his name is a perpetual reminder that God promises the impossible and keeps His promises.
- Finally, as the obedient son of the promise, Isaac prefigures Jesus Christ, the promised Son of God. He walked willingly and obediently up the hill to be sacrificed, even as Christ would so many years later. His life is a living testimony to

the God "who gives life to the dead and calls into existence the things that do not exist" (Rom. 4:17). He is the loving son and father and husband, the obedient son through whom God pours His blessing on a nation and on the world.

Lesson Summary

✔ Abraham continued to show faith that God would take an active role in establishing his family when he sent his servant to obtain a wife for Isaac from among his people.

✔ God chose Rebekah, a woman who was ready to leave her home for a strange land and the unknown husband. God chose for her to become the mother of the patriarch of the future nation of Israel.

✔ God's blessing fell on Isaac after Abraham's death.

✔ Just as He chose Isaac over his older brother Ishmael, God chose Isaac's younger son Jacob to succeed him as patriarch. He revealed to Rebekah that she was bearing twins who would always be at odds and that the younger would be stronger than and served by the elder. This illustrates the principle of election, whereby God chooses not based on natural birthright or man's effort or deeds, but on His sovereign will and mercy.

✔ The fact that Rebekah and Jacob schemed and lied to get that blessing does not mean God approved their methods. Yet God in His sovereignty is able to use all actions for good and to further His purpose.

✔ Did Jacob wonder whether the blessing he tricked Isaac into giving would "stick"? Fleeing from Esau's wrath, Jacob received a wonderful confirmation in a dream from God Himself. God revealed Himself personally to Jacob, promising to fulfill through Jacob the blessings He had promised Abraham, and said He would never leave Jacob before accomplishing what He promised. Jacob would no longer be in Canaan, but God would always be with Jacob.

For responses to Lesson 8 questions, see pp. 154-56.

Jacob, the Patriarch of Israel
(Genesis 29-36)

Jacob was called by God to father His people. He had received both birthright and blessing from Isaac, and the blessing of Abraham had been passed down to him. But except for the dream he had before he left Canaan, Jacob knew God only as the Lord, the God of his father, Isaac, and of his grandfather, Abraham. What would it take to make the Lord his God, and to make him the father of God's people? Would he be tested as his forefathers were?

For Abraham, the test had been a test of his faith in God's word: Would he obey God and offer his beloved son on an altar? Did he really trust all the promises God had made?

Isaac had been tested in his self-sacrificing obedience: Would the promised son willingly submit to his father's plan to sacrifice him? When he was an adult, would he obey God and stay in Canaan, even when that was hard to do?

Jacob's testing would occur in the crucible of life. Stealing the blessing from his brother had been easy. When more obstacles came his way, how hard would he work to hang onto that blessing? Jacob knew before he ever left Canaan that someday he would have to return and face his brother. Would he have the courage to do that when God told him the time had come? Jacob had vowed to make God his own, after his dramatic dream about the ladder. When he finally returns to Canaan, will we see any difference in him?

This lesson will cover Genesis 29–36. Much of it will be summarized, without any specific questions to answer.

"He Opened to Us the Scriptures"

Before we read God's Word, we ought to take a moment to humble ourselves before Him, remembering that His Word is primarily a conversation with us, not a textbook. "Speak, Lord, for thy servant hears" (1 Sam. 3:9) can be the prayer on our lips. Then, read all the way through Genesis 32:1–33:11 and 35:1–15. Think about what you understand and what you don't understand. Make a simple response to God in terms of what you do understand. Write your prayer in this space:

_____

_____

_____

_____

_____

Now, ask for His help as you work on the questions below.
(Prayer hint: "*Lord, let me not forget that You are always with me, even when I cannot see or hear You.*")

❧

Questions

Summary of Genesis 29–31

Jacob went to find a wife in Haran among Rebekah's people. Almost immediately he fell in love with a woman named Rachel, a daughter of Laban, Rebekah's brother. Jacob offered to serve Laban for seven years in order to obtain Rachel as his wife. Laban agreed to his proposal, but Jacob got a dose of his own medicine from the wily Laban. He who, back in Canaan, had stolen the benefits of the firstborn by pretending to be the elder, got not Rebekah but Leah, the first-born daughter, who pretended to be the younger! Just as Rachel substituted her younger son for the older to achieve her goal, her brother Laban substituted his older daughter for the younger. "It is not so done in our country," Laban told Jacob, "to give the younger before the first-born" (Gen. 29:26). The deceiver had himself been deceived.

Life was never easy for Jacob in the land away from Canaan. From his two wives (and their concubines), Jacob fathered eleven sons and a daughter. The family dynamic was tense and competitive between the wives. Jacob loved Rachel, not Leah, which created a festering wound in the bosom of the family. In addition, although Jacob worked hard for Laban, making him rich, Laban cheated Jacob at every turn.

Nevertheless, Jacob prospered. Eventually he desired to return to the land of Canaan, but the sons of Laban, who were jealous of his amazing success at everything he touched, tried to thwart him. They poisoned Laban's mind against him. God appeared to Jacob again in a dream: "I am the God of Bethel, where you anointed a pillar and made a vow to me. Now arise, go forth from this land, and return to the land of your birth" (Gen. 31:13). Jacob was ready to listen to God's command because he was confident of His care. He told his wives: "I see that your father does not regard me with favor as he did before. But the God of my father has been with me. You know that I have served your father with all my strength; yet your father has cheated me and changed my wages ten times, but God did not permit him to harm me" (Gen. 31:5–7).

Jacob packed up his wives, children, servants, and possessions and fled during the night. Laban's daughters were bitter towards their father, because he had also cheated them out of their inheritance. Out of spite, Rachel stole her father's household gods and packed them into her camel's saddle. Laban went in hot pursuit of the entourage, but his wrath was turned away when God appeared to him in a dream, saying, "Take heed that you say not a word to Jacob, either good or bad" (Gen. 31:24). When Laban caught up with Jacob, his son-in-law spoke passionately of Laban's cruelty and God's goodness: "These twenty years I have been in your house; I served you fourteen years for your two daughters, and six years for your flock, and you have changed my wages ten times. If the God of my father, the God of Abraham and the Fear of Isaac, had not been on my side, surely now you would have sent me away empty-handed. God saw my affliction and the labor of my hands, and rebuked you last night" (Gen. 31:41–42). Laban was pacified, and the family dispute was settled amiably. Jacob was finally able to focus all his energy on his biggest challenge yet: facing Esau.

Jacob Heads Home

📖 Read Genesis 32:1–21.

1. Think back to the circumstances that led to Jacob's flight from Canaan.

a. What kind of reception might he have expected from his brother Esau?

_____

_____

_____

_____

b. What immediate assurance did Jacob get that God was with him (vv. 1–3)?

_____

_____

_____

_____

c. However Jacob hoped Esau might receive him, he was clearly distressed by Esau's response. The last time Esau came after him, Jacob fled. Even though he was afraid, how did Jacob respond this time (vv. 7–21)?

_____

_____

_____

_____

d. What do you think explains the difference in the Jacob who left Canaan and the Jacob who returned?

_____

_____

_____

_____

A New Name and a Blessing

𝄞 **Read Genesis 32:22–32.**

2. Having earnestly prayed for deliverance from Esau (Gen. 32:9–12), and having done all he could to appease his brother, Jacob settled down alone for the night. Then something odd happened: "And a man wrestled with him until the breaking of the day" (v. 24). Although the narrative of this incident is spare of the kind of details we'd love to have, it is of vital importance in our study of Jacob and the nation he fathered.

a. Jacob wrestled with a mysterious "man" who appeared out of nowhere. When they first began their struggle, who might Jacob have suspected this "man" to be?

_____

_____

_____

_____

b. The struggle lasted all night. The "man" could not prevail over Jacob, so with a simple "touch" of the hollow of his thigh, Jacob's thigh was put out of joint. What would that "touch" have revealed to Jacob about the identity of this "man" (see also v. 26)?

_____

_____

_____

_____

c. Jacob had prayed to God for deliverance in facing Esau (vv. 11–12). In that prayer, Jacob reminded God of His promise "to do [him] good." When Jacob realized who this "man" was, what might have been his justifiable reaction to the way God answered his prayer for deliverance and for the "good" He had promised?

_____

_____

_____

_____

d. In spite of how he might have reacted to this mysterious wrestler, how did Jacob respond to the "man" (v. 26)?

_____

_____

_____

3. The "man" asked Jacob his name, although, of course, he already knew it.

a. Why do you suppose he asked anyway?

_____

_____

_____

_____

b. The "man" then changed Jacob's name to "Israel," which means "he who strives with God." Why do you think God changed Jacob's name at this point in the episode?

_____

_____

_____

_____

c. Jacob asked the "man" his name. Look at the answer he got in verse 29. What do you think the "man" meant by his evasive response to Jacob's question? Also see Exodus 3:13–14 and the *Catechism*, nos. 205–6.

_____

_____

_____

_____

4. Look at the name Jacob gave that spot of earth in verse 30. What does the name tell us about what Jacob understood about his mysterious wrestling match that night?

_____

_____

_____

_____

_____

Israel: He Who Strives with God

"Israel" became the name of the nation God had promised to Abraham and his descendants. What would this episode in Jacob's life, and the name that came from it, have taught them about their destiny as God's chosen people?

The nation that bore the name "Israel" should have understood that in their relationship with God, they would have to strive with Him in order to receive the blessing He promised them, just as Jacob had done. God and Israel would be like wrestlers, who sometimes look like they are locked in a lovers' embrace and at other times like they are in combat to the death. Abraham's descendants would need to know that God was on their side no matter what the circumstances looked like. He was ready to give them a blessing if only they persevered, seeking Him with courage and determination, as Jacob had done. In fact, even when God inflicted pain on them, as He had done on Jacob's thigh, they would have to trust that it was worth it to continue clinging to Him and refuse to let go. They would need to remember the deep pleasure God received from Jacob's tenacious faith, which moved Him to change his name.

To be called by the name "Israel" was a high calling. Only one Son of Israel fulfilled it perfectly—Jesus. Jacob's wrestling match with God foreshadowed Christ on the Cross, when He persevered through death ("My God, My God, why hast Thou forsaken Me?") to glory ("Into Thy hands I commend My Spirit."), obtaining God's blessing not for Himself but for us.

Israel's destiny was all in a Name.

Jacob Confronts Esau

≯ **Read Genesis 33:1–11.**

5. As Jacob approached his brother, what was the first thing he wanted Esau to understand about this encounter, even as he saw Jacob from a distance (v. 3)?

_____
_____
_____
_____
_____

6. The reunion of the two brothers was emotional.

a. The last time Esau had seen Jacob, he vowed to kill him. What do you suppose explains his great happiness over their reunion?

_____
_____
_____
_____

b. The last time Jacob and Esau had lived together, Esau had sold something to Jacob (his birthright), and Jacob had cheated Esau of something (his blessing). In their reunion, the subject of possessions and ownership came up, but how was it radically different this time (vv. 9–11)?

_____
_____
_____
_____

7. *Challenge question*: Jacob made an amazing statement to Esau in verse 10: "to see your face is like seeing the face of God." What do you think he meant?

_____

_____

_____

_____

Summary of Genesis 33:12–34:31

After the reunion with Esau, Jacob journeyed on into the land of Canaan. Instead of returning to Bethel, where he had made his vow to God, he settled his family in the city of Shechem, where he bought some land and erected an altar. He called that place El-Elohe-Israel, which meant, "God, the God of Israel" (Gen. 33:20). We see in this name that Jacob claimed God as his very own, but he still had a long way to go in learning to actually live the truth that he professed in worship.

Almost immediately upon their arrival in Shechem, trouble flared up for Jacob's family. His only daughter, Dinah, was raped by a prince of the land, named Shechem. Although it had been a crime of lust, the prince's "soul was drawn to Dinah, the daughter of Jacob; he loved the maiden and spoke to her tenderly" (Gen. 34:3). The prince asked his father, Hamor, to arrange their marriage with Jacob. This he did straight away, asking not only that Dinah be allowed to marry his son but also to "make marriages with us; give your daughters to us, and take our daughters for yourselves" (Gen. 34:9). Hamor hoped the offer of intermarriage with the family of Jacob seemed like an easy and direct path to great prosperity in the land of Shechem.

However, the sons of Jacob were furious over the rape of Dinah. They believed the family had been insulted and humiliated. Curiously, Jacob deferred to his sons in his handling of the problem: "Jacob heard that [Shechem] had defiled his daughter, Dinah, but . . . he held his peace until [his sons] came" (Gen. 34:5). The sons, driven by their anger, dealt deceitfully with Hamor and Shechem. They agreed to give their sister in marriage on the condition that all the Shechemites be circumcised. These strangers would have to bear the mark of Abraham's covenant with God in order for marriages to take place between the two families.

Hamor and Shechem agreed to this requirement. All the males of the city were circumcised, but as they were recovering, "when they were sore" (Gen. 34:25), two of Jacob's sons, Simeon and Levi, led a raid on them and killed all the males. They took Dinah and plundered the city, leaving nothing of value behind. Jacob was greatly disturbed by their treachery, but mostly because of the trouble it would cause for them with the other people of the land who heard about it: "You have brought trouble on me by making me odious to the inhabitants of the land" (Gen. 34:30). Simeon and Levi were unrepentant, however: "Should he treat our sister as a harlot?" (Gen. 34:31).

Return to Bethel
※ Read Genesis 35:1–15.
8. God spoke to Jacob in the middle of this tragic situation.
a. God told Jacob to go to Bethel and make an altar there. Before packing up for the journey, Jacob addressed his household. Look at verses 2–4. Why do you suppose Jacob gave these instructions to his family?

_____

_____

_____

_____

b. *Challenge question*: Look at verses 9–15. When Jacob and his family arrived at Bethel, God repeated many of the significant details of His call to Jacob, His promises to him, and Jacob's earlier responses. This repetition helps us to understand the reason God sent Jacob back to Bethel. What was it?

_____

_____

_____

_____

Summary of Genesis 35:16–36:43
From Bethel, Jacob traveled to Ephrath, where Rachel, his beloved wife, died in childbirth. The son she bore was named Benjamin. Thus, the sons of Jacob were twelve: Reuben, Simeon, Levi, Judah, Issachar, Zebulun, Joseph, Benjamin, Dan, Naphthali, Gad, and Asher. Added to the sorrow of losing his favorite wife, Jacob endured the offense of one of his sons, Reuben, sleeping with his concubine (incest of this sort, by a son with his father's wife or concubine, was always an act of prideful rebellion against the father rather than simple lust). Although Jacob had removed his family from potential trouble in Shechem, the consequences of earlier compromises and weaknesses in raising his children would be felt for a long time to come.

Isaac, the son of Abraham, died at the age of 180; both Jacob and Esau buried their father. Then Esau removed his family from the land of Canaan, effectively ceding the land to his younger brother, Jacob. This was done without rancor or a fight. Esau's descendants formed the nation of Edom, "in the hill country of Seir" (Gen. 36:8). Jacob and his family were left to fulfill the promise God made to Abraham: they settled into the land of Abraham's sojourning.

※

"Did Not Our Hearts Burn Within Us?"

Our hearts will burn with joy when we consciously open them wide to God's Word. Scripture memorization is a good way to get that started. Here is a suggested memory verse:

Your name shall no more be called Jacob, but Israel, for you have striven with God and with men, and have prevailed.

—Gen. 32:28

Continue to welcome Him into your soul by reflecting on these questions:

Jacob had a dramatic experience with God at Bethel, just as he left Canaan. He exchanged promises with Him, and he set off on a new chapter in his life. He might have thought his new personal relationship with God would mean success, good fortune, and an easy life in Haran. Instead, he got cheated, his wives were in constant turmoil, and his own brothers-in-law hated him. Life was hard in Haran. Nevertheless, his faith slowly grew. The hardship turned him towards God, not away.

Have you experienced a deepening in your life with God, only to be followed by one trial after another? Is there anything in Jacob's story that will help you to be thankful instead of resentful for all those bumps in the road?

_____

_____

_____

_____

_____

2. Is there anyone in your life from whom you are estranged, as Jacob was from Esau? Is it in your power to make the first move towards reconciliation? Can Jacob's bowing to the ground in plain sight of his brother inspire you to find a way to make things right?

_____

_____

_____

_____

_____

3. Jacob had to take charge of a family careening out of control. When he realized how little his sons understood the meaning of the covenant and its sign, circumcision, he asserted his moral authority over them and called them to purification. He removed bad influences and taught them something about worship, prayer, and God's faithfulness. He tried the best he could to make up for past shortcomings.

Jacob's example is helpful for families or individuals who find themselves in bad situations of their own making. Do you need a moral inventory in your family or personal life? Is purification in order? Can you make a fresh start with God?

_____

_____

_____

_____

_____

❧

"Stay with Us"

In the midst of the turmoil and selfishness that characterize Jacob's young household, it is tempting to step back and question God's wisdom in building His future kingdom on one man's family. Why not reach down and call out more Abrahams? Surely a nation better representative of God could be put together from separate, well-chosen individuals!

Perhaps. And yet there is something deeply significant about the fact that God started with a family. He began it all with Adam and Eve and the command to be fruitful and multiply: the first human family would be a reflection of the triune Family of God Himself. After the Fall, He made a fresh start with Noah and Noah's wife, their sons and their sons' wives: a family household. And now—even though we have seen time and time again that the righteousness of one man does not necessarily continue on in his children—God persisted in His plan to use the offspring of one righteous man to bless the world. Why?

Because salvation from sin and life with God is a family affair.

God used flawed families in Israel to teach us a significant lesson about the family He would one day create in the New Israel, the Church. In Baptism, we are "born again" into the family of God. Jesus, our Brother, made that possible for us. Are we weak? Do we stumble and lose our footing sometimes? Most definitely. Yet we can see that God loved His covenant family; He did not give up on them. Even when Jacob's family makes us cringe, we need to thank God that He was willing to continue calling them His people.

Mercifully, the Catholic Church preserves this sense of family. God is our Father. Mary is our Mother; the saints are our brothers and sisters. In the Church hierarchy, too, there are fathers and sisters and brothers. Think of the significance of our family prayer, the "Our Father." Because Christ has given us his nature, we can dare to call God "Father!" "Abba"—"Daddy." "See what love the Father has given us, that we should be called children of God; and so we are" (1 John 3:1). Thanks be to God!!

Lesson Summary

✔ God truly watched over Jacob when he left the land of Canaan, just as He had promised. Through all the struggles of Jacob's years in Haran, He accomplished His purpose to start a family that would form the basis of the new nation of Israel. God made Jacob a blessing to others, and He prepared him to return to the home he had to flee.

✔ As Jacob left Laban he was met by God's angelic army, a reminder of God's continued presence, care, and protection.

✔ God met Jacob in a mysterious way on the night before his entrance into Canaan. The two wrestled all night, and when Jacob realized the identity of "the man," he asked for a blessing. He got the blessing, as well as a new name—Israel. He learned that God delights in those who refuse to give up the search for a blessing from Him, even after experiencing crippling pain.

✔ Esau received Jacob with a changed heart: he was warm, generous, and forgiving. Jacob pressed on his brother a share in the bounty God had blessed him with, in some way a return on the blessing he stole from Esau many years before.

✔ Jacob's faith in God had grown considerably during his time in Haran. He built an altar to God as he journeyed toward Bethel and called it El-Elohe-Israel, "God the God of Israel" (Gen. 33:20). The God of his fathers had become his own.

✔ Instead of going all the way to Bethel, Jacob stopped in a town called Shechem. His daughter was raped, and his sons took violent revenge on the whole town. They used circumcision to accomplish their treachery.

✔ Jacob realized his sons needed his leadership if they were to be true descendants of Abraham. He had them get rid of the foreign idols in their home, put clean clothes on, and watch him worship God at an altar he built. God mercifully intervened and called Jacob back to Himself at Bethel. So Jacob moved his large family to Bethel, which was where God had directed him in the first place.

✔ Jacob's beloved wife Rachel died giving birth to Benjamin, leaving him with twelve sons who would father the nation of Israel.

✔ When the land could no longer support two growing tribes, Esau moved his family away from Jacob, who was left to inherit the Land of Promise.

For responses to Lesson 9 questions, see pp. 157-60.

Joseph's Rise to Power
(Genesis 37–41)

W e have been watching since we left the Garden of Eden to see how God would bring about reconciliation between mankind and Himself. We saw Him reach down and promise to bring blessing through the family of one man, Abraham, and we have watched that family grow. Jacob learned a significant lesson about how a man receives God's blessing in an all-night wrestling match. His new name, "Israel," or "he who strives with God," helped us to understand that to get God's blessing means perseverance, even in the face of the most difficult and contrary circumstances.

Jacob returned to Canaan, and he settled into his birthright as heir to the promises of God to Abraham. His family of twelve sons formed the foundation of the nation of Israel. But Jacob's sons were hardly poster boys for the budding chosen people. The firstborn, Reuben, challenged Jacob's authority by sleeping with his concubine. Simeon and Levi, sons two and three, made Jacob's name "odious" to his neighbors with their violent and bloody revenge of their sister's rape. How could such an unlikely bunch of people figure so prominently in God's plan for blessing? Watch closely, for the answer to the question of how God could save this family shows, in microcosm, what He would one day do to save the whole world.

"He Opened to Us the Scriptures"

Before we read God's Word, we ought to take a moment to humble ourselves before Him, remembering that His Word is primarily a conversation with us, not a textbook. "Speak, LORD, for thy servant hears" (1 Sam. 3:9) can be the prayer on our lips. Because there are several Scripture passages to examine in this lesson, we suggest that you meditate on the following verse as you begin this study:

The LORD was with Joseph, and he became a successful man; and he was in the house of his master the Egyptian, and his master saw that the LORD was

with him, and that the L<small>ORD</small> caused all that he did to prosper in his hands.
—Gen. 39:2–3

Make a simple response to God and write your prayer in this space:

_____

_____

_____

_____

_____

Now, ask for His help as you work on the questions below.

🔥

Questions
Joseph and His Dreams

🔥 **Read Genesis 37:1–11.**

[*Note: Variously translated "tunic with sleeves," "long robe with sleeves," and "richly ornamented robe," the Hebrew phrase describing Joseph's coat is used elsewhere to indicate a royal garment (see 2 Sam. 13:18). Its length and sleeves would make the wearer unfit for common labor.*]

1. Joseph, the second-to-youngest son of Jacob and his favorite wife, Rachel, had a complicated relationship with his older brothers. Read verses 1–4.

a. Why did Joseph's brothers hate him so much?

_____

_____

_____

_____

b. Did Joseph consciously provoke his brothers?

_____

_____

_____

_____

2. Joseph was a boy with unusual dreams. Read verses 5–11.

a. When his brothers and father heard about the dreams, what conclusion did they jump to?

_____

_____

_____

_____

b. What other conclusion might the dreams have suggested to Joseph's family?

_____

_____

_____

_____

The Plot against Joseph

✣ **Read Genesis 37:12–28.**

3. Jacob sent Joseph to check on his brothers and the flocks they pastured.

a. Look at verse 18. Why do you think the sight of Joseph, even "afar off, and before he came near to them" made his brothers conspire to kill him?

_____

_____

_____

_____

b. Look at verse 20. What lay at the heart of the bitterness the brothers felt for Joseph?

_____

_____

_____

_____

c. Reuben had a plan to rescue Joseph from the pit where his brothers tossed him. Look at verse 22. What lay at the heart of Reuben's plan?

_____

_____

_____

_____

4. When the brothers got hold of Joseph, they "stripped him of his robe" (v. 23) and cast him into a pit.

a. Why do you think stripping him of his robe was the first thing they did to him?

_____

_____

_____

_____

b. What do you think Joseph said or did while he was in that pit, as his brothers "sat down to eat" (v. 25)?

_____

_____

_____

_____

c. Why did Judah suggest selling Joseph to the Ishmaelites instead of killing him (vv. 26–27)?

_____

_____

_____

_____

"His Father Wept for Him"

🦅 **Read Genesis 37:29–36.**

5. Apparently, Reuben had not been with the brothers when they sold Joseph. Perhaps he had been tending the flocks. He was shocked to discover what had happened.

a. Why do you think the brothers used the robe that Jacob had given Joseph to deceive their father about Joseph's fate?

_____

_____

_____

_____

b. Jacob was comforted by "all his sons and all his daughters" (v. 35), but he continued to mourn for Joseph "many days." Why do you think the "comfort" of his other children had so little effect on him?

_____

_____

_____

_____

Summary of Genesis 38

Judah, one of Joseph's brothers, also left his father's home, but under very different circumstances from Joseph's departure. He wanted to marry and establish a household, so he took a wife, Shua, from among the Canaanites. He had three sons with her; the first one was so "wicked in the sight of the LORD" (v. 7) that "the LORD slew him." That son left behind a widow, Tamar, and according to the custom of the time, Judah told his second son, Onan, to father a child with his brother's widow, so she could "raise up offspring" in her husband's name.

Onan had sexual relations with Tamar, but rather than fathering a child for his brother (which was the purpose of the sexual union), "he spilled the semen on the ground" (v. 9). This angered the Lord, so He slew him. Judah sent Tamar home to her father, with the promise that when his youngest son, Shelah, was of age, he would do his duty by her. Judah did not keep his promise, because he

---

feared he would lose his third and only son. So Tamar disguised herself as a harlot and sat where Judah was sure to see her. Not knowing it was Tamar, his own daughter-in-law, he propositioned her. He gave her several personal items as pledge for the payment he would later send her, and then he lay with her. Tamar went back to her father's house, but she had conceived twins in this union.

Judah sought the "harlot" out to pay his debt, but no one had seen a harlot anywhere in the region. About three months later, Judah got word of Tamar's pregnancy. Still not realizing what he had done, he called for her death because his youngest son would have been the only licit father of her child, and he had not been given to her. Tamar sent to Judah the personal items he had given her, along with this word: "By the man to whom these belong, I am with child" (v. 25).

Judah was caught; he acknowledged what he had done and said, "'She is more righteous than I, inasmuch as I did not give her to my son, Shelah.' And he did not lie with her again" (v. 26). Tamar gave birth to Perez and Zerah; Perez was an ancestor of King David, who was an ancestor of Jesus.

What a sad story! Its details force us to face the fact that God's covenant with Abraham and his descendants was unshakable, even though there were weak and selfish people among them. Fortunately, there were good examples of covenant people among them, too. The position of this story here helps to form a contrast with what comes next. Judah, although a free man, used his freedom badly. Joseph was sold as a slave. What would he make of his captivity?

Joseph in Egypt

🦢 **Read Genesis 39:1–6a.**

6. Joseph was bought by Potiphar, an officer of Pharaoh, and he had an extremely successful career in his home. What did Potiphar recognize in Joseph that his brothers back home in Canaan had never understood?

_____

_____

Joseph and Potiphar's Wife

🦢 **Read Genesis 39:7–23.**

7. Joseph was preyed upon by his master's wife.

a. We don't know whether Joseph was attracted to the woman or not, but why did he absolutely refuse to lie with her?

_____

_____

_____

b. The woman made false charges against Joseph. Why do you think he spoke not a word in his defense?

_____

_____

_____

_____

8. Although it must have been awful for Joseph to know that he was imprisoned falsely and that his master, whom he had served so well, thought of him as a betrayer (v. 19), what was his life like in prison?

_____

_____

_____

_____

_____

Summary of Genesis 40–41:13

Joseph was joined in prison by two other men who had offended the Pharaoh. One was the king's butler, the other the king's baker. They were in Joseph's care, and one day he found both of them very troubled. He asked them, "Why are your faces downcast today?" (v. 7). They told him about disturbing dreams each of them had the night before, but they had no idea what they meant. Joseph said to them, "Do not interpretations belong to God? Tell them to me, I pray you" (v. 8).

Joseph was able to accurately interpret both their dreams. The butler was to be restored to his position with the king, but the baker was to lose his head. Joseph asked the butler to "do me the kindness, I pray you, to make mention of me to Pharaoh, and so get me out of this house, for I was indeed stolen out of the land of the Hebrews; and here also I have done nothing that they should put me into the dungeon" (vv. 14–15).

The butler, unfortunately, forgot all about Joseph when his dream became reality, and he was restored to the king's court. Two years passed. Then Pharaoh himself had several dreams that deeply troubled him, because he did not understand them. "He sent and called for all the magicians of Egypt and all its wise men; and Pharaoh told them his dreams, but there was none who could interpret [them] to Pharaoh" (v. 8).

Then the butler remembered Joseph. He told Pharaoh about the Hebrew servant in prison who had been able to accurately interpret dreams. Joseph's day had finally arrived.

Pharaoh's Dreams

🕯 **Read Genesis 41:14–45.**

9. Two full years had passed since Joseph asked the chief butler to remember him to Pharaoh. Undoubtedly this seemed a long time to Joseph; yet the butler's forgetfulness turned out to be a boon for Joseph. By forgetting until Pharaoh's unsolved dreams reminded him, his report came at a time when Joseph stood to make the greatest gain from it: not only release from prison, but a new position of power.

   a. What did Joseph's response when Pharaoh asked him to interpret his dreams (v. 16) reveal about Joseph?

_____

_____

_____

_____

   b. Look at the gifts and authority Pharaoh bestowed on Joseph, described in verses 39–45. Do you think any of it reminded Joseph of his life in Canaan?

_____

_____

_____

_____

Joseph, Ruler in Egypt

🕯 **Read Genesis 41:46–57.**

10. Joseph was exceedingly successful, again, in his work for Pharaoh.

   a. Look at the names Joseph gave his two sons in verses 51–52. What do they tell us about the man Joseph had become?

_____

_____

_____

_____

"What he says to you, do"

When the famine in Egypt grew severe, the people cried out to Pharaoh for bread. It was a measure of Joseph's authority and power that the Pharaoh's response to this cry was, "Go to Joseph; what he says to you, do" (vs. 55).

How reminiscent these words are of another shortage, nearly two thousand years later. At a wedding in Cana, there was no wine. After informing Jesus about the shortage, Mary spoke to the servants in attendance at the wedding: "Do whatever He tells you" (John 2:5).

---

b. *Challenge question*: When Pharaoh appointed Joseph second-in-command, he undoubtedly was thinking of the good Joseph would do for Egypt. Do you see any evidence that God had bigger plans in mind (v. 57)?

_____

_____

_____

_____

❧

"Did Not Our Hearts Burn Within Us?"

Our hearts will burn with joy when we consciously open them wide to God's Word. Scripture memorization is a good way to get that started. Here is a suggested memory verse:

> *The LORD was with Joseph, and he became a successful man; and he was in the house of his master the Egyptian, and his master saw that the LORD was with him, and that the LORD caused all that he did to prosper in his hands.*
>
> *—Gen. 39:2–3*

Continue to welcome Him into your soul by reflecting on these questions:

The story of the jealousy of Joseph's brothers is painful to read. We could say that Jacob was partly responsible for it because of his favoritism, singling out one son for special love. We could say that Joseph was partly responsible for it, because his goodness made his brothers look bad. In the end, the brothers themselves were really responsible for it. They should not have begrudged an old man his love; they should not have begrudged their brother his virtue.

Do you struggle sometimes with jealousy? Do you easily find good reasons to justify it? Can the sad details of the story of jealousy in this lesson encourage you to mortify, not justify, it whenever it pops up in your life?

_____

_____

_____

_____

_____

What amazes us about Joseph was his ability not to allow the misery and pain he undoubtedly felt over his various misfortunes—being sold as a slave, being falsely condemned and imprisoned, being forgotten—to paralyze him. In each new set of circumstances in his life, even though he hadn't chosen them, he had something to contribute. He made the best of each situation, not wasting time in anger or sorrow over what was wrong. He could live that way because he knew, increasingly, that God was with him.

And so do we. There isn't anything that can happen to us that will separate us from the love of God. Is that a truth you really need to hear today? Can Joseph's example help you to make the most of even the worst in your life?

_____

_____

_____

_____

_____

❧

"Stay with Us"

As we follow the engaging details of Joseph's life story, it doesn't take long for us to ask, "Who is this guy?" His virtue isn't like anything we've seen in Genesis so far. His amazing confidence in God, his humble acceptance of all his circumstances, his resistance to temptation, his service to others, even in prison, his spiritual discernment, and his overwhelming competence set him in a category all his own. He stands head and shoulders above nearly everyone who came before him. What can this mean?

The life of Joseph is a remarkable Old Testament picture of how God would one day use a descendant of Abraham to restore blessing to the whole world, just as He promised in Genesis 12:1–3. Joseph, one of Jacob's twelve sons, was most extraordinarily blessed. How unlike his brothers he was! His life was graced in every way by God's protection and presence. Joseph barely seems human sometimes. Indeed, his brothers hated and envied him, wanting him dead. Yet through his "death" in the pit and his sojourn in Egypt, he was elevated to a position of authority and grandeur second only to Pharaoh himself. Although he had been sold for a handful of shekels, he distributed bread to the starving world. Joseph always knew the hand of God was upon him, even in his childhood dreams. He was able to endure exile to a foreign land, false charges and imprisonment, and the forgetfulness of a close associate without turning bitter, desperate, or vengeful. Wherever he went, whatever he faced, he did good to others.

Would there ever be another man like him? Yes! Joseph would join the patriarchs and prophets who point to the One who was promised. What else can Joseph teach us about the One who is to come? More than we could ever imagine.

Lesson Summary

✔ Jacob's preference for Joseph aroused envy in his other sons, which turned to hate when they heard of Joseph's dreams that they would bow to him one day.

✔ Unwilling to see those dreams come to pass, Joseph's brothers first plotted to kill the boy and then sold him into slavery.

✔ While Joseph was taken off to Egypt, Judah went to Canaan and married a Canaanite woman. God killed his first two sons for their wickedness. Judah's attempt to save his third son might have cost him future generations except for Tamar's resourcefulness, when she tricked Judah into lying with her. It would be their son who fathered the line from which Christ would eventually come.

✔ God was with Joseph in slavery in Egypt and blessed him through it, prospering him and giving him success, with the result that Potiphar, his master, gave Joseph complete charge over his household.

✔ In contrast to Judah, Joseph resisted temptation and kept his eyes on God. He was a true model of strength in the face of temptation, of humble acceptance of God's will, and of faith in the face of difficult circumstances.

✔ Thrown from his high position in Potiphar's household into prison on unjust charges, Joseph soon rose to responsibility there as well. Joseph correctly interpreted the dreams of two men in his care. Joseph asked the one who was eventually freed to remember him before Pharaoh.

✔ Any hopes Joseph had for a quick release dissolved as the chief butler forgot to speak on his behalf. But God was with Joseph and blessed him both in and through his trials, not removing him from the bad situations but using them to effect good and to further His purposes.

✔ After two years of humble obedience, Joseph was lifted to a position from which he could save Egypt (and the countries around it) from famine. Thus God continued His plan to bless the world through a son of Abraham.

For responses to Lesson 10 questions, see pp. 160-63.

Reconciliation and Reunion
(Genesis 42–45)

In Joseph, the eleventh son of Jacob, we finally found someone who acted the way we expect a descendant of Abraham, a son of the covenant, to act. In contrast to nearly all the other sons of Jacob, who were self-serving, rebellious, and dishonest, Joseph was honest and hardworking, patient in suffering, and trusting in God. He was a man who was tempted, but who strove not to sin. He was humbled, but God exalted him. He who was once stripped of everything and became a servant was eventually raised up to keep a starving world alive.

Does any of this sound familiar?

Joseph's resemblance to Jesus has become unmistakable. Their histories parallel each other in a most remarkable way. As we press on into Joseph's story, we will want to watch carefully what happens when Joseph, the beloved son of his father, faces once again the brothers who betrayed them. How can such a troubled family be reconciled? What will their story teach us about how mankind, God's troubled family, can be reconciled to Him?

"He Opened to Us the Scriptures"

Before we read God's Word, we ought to take a moment to humble ourselves before Him, remembering that His Word is primarily a conversation with us, not a textbook. "Speak, LORD, for thy servant hears" (1 Sam. 3:9) can be the prayer on our lips. Because there are several Scripture passages to examine in this lesson, we suggest that you meditate on the following verse as you begin this study:

> *And God sent me before you to preserve for you a remnant on earth, and to keep alive for you many survivors. So it was not you who sent me here, but God.*
> —*Gen. 45:7–8*

Make a simple response to God and write your prayer in this space:

_____

_____

_____

_____

_____

Now, ask for His help as you work on the questions below.

❧

Questions
Famine in the Land of Canaan

❧ **Read Genesis 42:1–5.**

1. The famine was severe in Canaan, so Jacob decided to send ten of his sons to Egypt to buy grain. He held back Benjamin, Joseph's brother and the only remaining son of Rachel, "for he feared that harm might befall him" (v. 4).

a. What does this reserve about Benjamin tell us about Jacob?

_____

_____

_____

_____

b. What does Jacob's reserve about Benjamin suggest to us about the other ten brothers?

_____

_____

_____

_____

Jacob's Sons Go Down to Egypt

❧ **Read Genesis 42: 6–25.**

[**Note**: *At least twenty years had passed since Joseph had seen his brothers, yet he recognized them. The change had been greater in Joseph, who was just seventeen when they last met, than in the others, who had been men already. Even had they expected to see Joseph, it would not have been as the governor of the land, looking like an Egyptian and speaking through an interpreter.*]

2. Joseph's brothers appeared before him "and bowed themselves before him with their faces to the ground" (v. 6). Joseph immediately recognized them, but they did not know him.

a. *Challenge question*: Joseph recalled his dreams about his brothers, fulfilled before his eyes. What might that have suggested to him about his long, difficult sojourn in Egypt?

_____
_____
_____
_____

b. If Joseph's heart had been full of anger and revenge, what could he have done to his brothers?

_____
_____
_____
_____

c. *Challenge question*: Why do you think Joseph "treated them like strangers and spoke roughly to them" (v. 7), accusing them of being spies?

_____
_____
_____

3. In response to Joseph's accusation that they were spies, his brothers insisted they were "sons of one man" and "honest" (v. 11). When Joseph discovered that his brother, Benjamin, was still alive, he quickly developed a plan to test both their integrity and their sonship.

    a. Joseph put all the brothers in prison for "three days" (v. 17). What happened to them while they were there (vv. 21–22)?

_____
_____
_____
_____

    b. Look at Joseph's reaction to the brothers' conversation in verse 24. What do you think provoked it?

_____
_____
_____
_____

    c. Joseph demanded the brothers get Benjamin and return to Egypt. Although he "took Simeon [as surety] from them and bound him before their eyes" (v. 24), he also, unbeknownst to the brothers, returned to their bags all the money they had spent buying grain (v. 25). Why do you suppose he did that?

_____
_____
_____

Summary of Genesis 42:26–43:10

Joseph's brothers departed for Canaan, and when they stopped along the way, they discovered all the money had been returned to their bags. "At this their hearts failed them, and they turned trembling to one another, saying, 'What is this that God has done to us?'" (Gen. 42:28). They could not imagine what explained it, and it made them fearful. Everything associated with their trip to Egypt to buy grain had become bizarre and unpredictable.

When the brothers arrived at Jacob's home, they told him all that had happened. They referred to Joseph as "the man, the lord of the land." They told Jacob why they had left Simeon behind and that they needed to return with Benjamin to prove they weren't spies.

Jacob was overwhelmed by all the bad news, and he was none too happy with his sons, especially after seeing the returned money in their sacks. Although we are not told explicitly in the text, he must have wondered whether they had actually sold Simeon while they were in Egypt and whether they also planned to sell Benjamin. Jacob cried out, "You have bereaved me of my children: Joseph is no more, and Simeon is no more, and now you would take Benjamin; all this has come upon me" (Gen. 42:36). Even when Reuben offered the life of his own two sons as surety for Benjamin, Jacob refused to let him go.

The famine was severe, however, and eventually the grain bought in Egypt ran out. Jacob told the brothers to return for more, but Judah reminded him of what "the man" had required of them. Judah promised his father that he would be fully responsible for Benjamin: "If I do not bring him back to you and set him before you, then let me bear the blame forever" (Gen. 43:9). There was no time to waste.

The Brothers Return to Egypt

🎺 Read Genesis 43:11–15.

4. Jacob (or "Israel" as in v. 11) finally agreed to let the brothers take Benjamin to Egypt.

a. Look at Genesis 42:36–38 and 43:11–14. What was the noticeable difference between Jacob's two responses to the need for Benjamin to go to Egypt with his brothers?

_____

_____

_____

_____

b. *Challenge question*: What do you think changed his mind and his attitude about it?

_____

_____

_____

A Meal with Joseph

✵ **Read Genesis 43:16–25.**

5. The brothers were invited to dine with Joseph when they got to Egypt (v. 16).
   a. What was their reaction to this news (vv. 18–23)?

_____

_____

_____

b. Why do you think Joseph extended this invitation to his brothers?

_____

_____

_____

A Time to Make Merry

✵ **Read Genesis 43:26–34.**

6. Joseph could not contain the emotion he felt at seeing Benjamin (v. 30–31).
   a. The portions Joseph heaped up for Benjamin at the dinner table were "five times as many" as any of the brothers. What was so amazing about the brothers' reaction to this obvious favoritism (v. 34)?

_____

_____

_____

_____

b. Why do you think Joseph did not yet reveal his identity to his brothers?

_____

_____

_____

_____

Summary of Genesis 44:1–17

Joseph was delighted to see Benjamin again, but there was more he wanted to do in his family. He told his steward to fill the brothers' sacks with food and their money, as before, but this time the steward was to plant in Benjamin's bag

---

111

a silver cup that belonged to Joseph. After the brothers departed for Canaan, Joseph sent his steward after them, to charge them with robbery.

When the steward caught up with the brothers, they insisted on their innocence. They told the steward to search all their bags: "With whomever of your servants it be found, let him die, and we also will be my lord's slaves" (v. 9). The steward searched the bags and found the cup with Benjamin. Rather than accuse Benjamin of wrongdoing or saying to the steward, "Take him; he's yours," so that they could continue on their way, the brothers did an amazing thing: "every man loaded his ass, and they returned to the city" (v. 13).

When the brothers appeared before Joseph, Judah told him that all the brothers would be his slaves, not just Benjamin. Joseph refused this offer. He wanted only Benjamin in his service; the others were free to return to their father in peace.

Judah and Joseph

Read Genesis 44:18–45:3.

7. After Joseph said, "Go up in peace to your father" (v. 17), Judah stepped up to have a private word with him about Benjamin.

a. Why was Judah willing to take Benjamin's place as a slave to Joseph?

_____

_____

_____

_____

b. *Challenge question*: Why do you think it was at this moment that Joseph finally revealed his identity to his brothers?

_____

_____

_____

_____

A Joyful Reunion

Read Genesis 45:4–15.

8. Joseph's brothers were shocked into speechlessness by Joseph's revelation.

a. What was Joseph's first concern for them (v. 5)?

_____

_____

_____

_____

b. Why was Joseph able to be so forgiving of his brothers (vv. 7–8)? (Also see the *Catechism*, no. 312.)

_____

_____

_____

_____

c. What was it that Joseph most earnestly desired for his family (vv. 9–13)?

_____

_____

_____

_____

d. What evidence do we have in this episode that Joseph's longing would be satisfied (vv. 14–15)?

_____

_____

_____

_____

Summary of Genesis 45:16–28

A report of the arrival of Joseph's brothers reached Pharaoh. He was delighted with the news and made a generous offer to them: "Do this: take wagons from the land of Egypt for your little ones and for your wives, and bring your father, and come. Give no thought to your goods, for the best of all the land of Egypt is yours" (vv. 19–20).

Joseph sent his brothers back to Canaan with great provisions. As they departed, he said to them, "Do not quarrel on the way" (v. 24). He was ever solicitous of his family's well-being and harmony. When they arrived in Canaan and told Jacob the news that Joseph was still alive and was a great ruler in Egypt, "his heart fainted, for he did not believe them" (v. 26). They were able to convince him that the news was true, and Jacob resolved to make the trip to Egypt: "Joseph my son is alive; I will go and see him before I die" (v. 28).

"Did Not Our Hearts Burn Within Us?"

Our hearts will burn with joy when we consciously open them wide to God's Word. Scripture memorization is a good way to get that started. Here is a suggested memory verse:

And God sent me before you to preserve for you a remnant on earth, and to keep alive for you many survivors. So it was not you who sent me here, but God.

—Gen. 45:7–8

Continue to welcome Him into your soul by reflecting on these questions:

When calamity overcame Joseph's brothers, and they were thrown in prison for "three days," they had both time and occasion to think back over their lives. When they acknowledged that they had sinned against Joseph, they were able to emerge from the darkness of the jail as new men. Humility replaced pride, and the family restoration could slowly begin.

None of us want that kind of experience, of course, but sometimes it happens. We find ourselves unexpectedly in scary circumstances. As painful as that can be, can you benefit from the story of Joseph's brothers if it happens to you? Can you remember to use the occasion to review your life? If some sin prods your conscience, can you make your way to the sacrament of Reconciliation? Can you make a fresh start from a dark time?

_____

_____

_____

_____

_____

How helpful it is for us to see in Joseph's story that appearances can be deceiving. Although Joseph looked like a cruel, demanding ruler to his brothers, behind all the rough talk was an ocean of love. He simply wanted his brothers to be true brothers to each other and true sons to their father. He had to be severe with them first, in order to purify them. Then they could enjoy rich family happiness.

Jesus can sometimes appear like Joseph in our lives. His Body, the Church, can as well. He asks a great deal of us—sometimes almost the impossible. When the call to holiness as a Catholic seems too difficult, does it help you to know that behind the appearance is an ocean of Love that simply seeks true joy for us as children of God and brothers to each other?

_____

_____

_____

_____

_____

Although he resisted it at first, Jacob finally accepted God's will as he said, "If I am bereaved of my children, I am bereaved." When he relinquished them into God's hands, he was able to move forward. Those steps he took started the process by which his children were returned to him. Is there anything you need to let go of to allow God to work in your life? Can Israel's example of surrender make a difference for you today?

_____

_____

_____

_____

_____

❦

"Stay with Us"

As Genesis began with a rupture in the relationship between man and God, it is fitting that the book draws to a close with a picture of the way God would one day heal that relationship by sending His Son to bring forgiveness and reconciliation. Joseph was in many ways a forerunner of Jesus, and the deeper we dig, the more parallels we find between him and the Messiah. A few are offered here for your consideration. Pondering them can enrich both our study of Joseph and our understanding of Jesus' work on our behalf.

Joseph and Jesus were alike:

—*in person and in character*:

- Both Joseph and Jesus were greatly loved by their fathers and envied and hated by their brothers.
- They were meek and humble, forgiving, compassionate, faithful in the face of opposition; they both faced temptation yet without sin.
- They neither condemned those who wronged them nor sought vengeance or personal apologies, but left judgment to God.
- They both graciously "paid" for the gift of life for their brethren—Joseph by returning bread money into his brothers' sacks and Jesus by offering His life on Calvary in place of sinners.
- They both forgave unconditionally. Their actions were motivated by love. They both threw feasts while in disguise to commune with their brethren.
- Both Joseph and Jesus set their eyes firmly on God and did not allow the way things appeared to distract them or cause them to doubt.
- Joseph had special affection for the brother who shared his own mother, Rachel; Jesus had special affection for His followers by sharing with them His own Mother, Mary.

—*in suffering and in glory*:

- Betrayed by those close to them, both were wrongly accused, stripped of their garments, and given over to die.
- They were each sold for a few pieces of silver into the hands of Gentiles.
- Joseph—like Jesus—lost all his rights and privileges and became a servant,

from which position God lifted him to a place of sovereignty at the king's right hand, where every knee bowed to him.
- Joseph was brought forth to life from the well and from prison; Jesus was brought forth to life from the tomb. After rising, neither was recognized by his brethren.

—and in their mission:
- God highly favored Joseph, above his brothers, in order that he would one day be able to save them and the nations from starvation's death. Through Joseph's "rough talk" and testing, his brothers were brought to repentance and reconciliation, with him and with their father; the family of Abraham was restored.
- God's Beloved Son, Jesus, was sent into the world to save all men from sin's death. By His preaching of the kingdom of God, much of which was "rough talk" (dying to self, plucking out an offending eye, selling all possessions, etc.) and testing ("unless your righteousness exceeds that of the Pharisees, you will never enter the kingdom of God," Mt. 5:20), men are brought to repentance and reconciliation, with their heavenly Father and each other; the family of God is restored.
- Both suffered so that others could live.
- Joseph, like Jesus, was able to save those who came to him and was the source of food that brings life.
- Joseph's life prepares us in a wonderful way for how God, in Jesus, kept His promise to bless the whole world through a descendant of Abraham.

Lesson Summary

✔ When Joseph's brothers went to Egypt for food they ended up bowing before Joseph, unwittingly bringing his early dreams to pass. Ironically, the very thing they thought would put an end to his dreams—selling him into slavery—God used to fulfill them.

✔ Joseph did not take advantage of his position over his brothers to get back at them; rather he used it to bless, returning their money and giving them provisions for their journey. Concealing his identity, Joseph used the situation and his position to test his brothers. As a result they were forced to examine their consciences regarding their treatment of Joseph while they were in prison for three days.

✔ In the process of carrying out Joseph's demands, Jacob's sons showed a new respect and honesty toward their father. A transformation took place in Judah, who took full responsibility for his father's loss and grief to the point of offering himself in place of Simeon and Benjamin should they return without them.

✔ A transformation was evident in Jacob as well, who came from the depths of despair to take his eyes off his problems and set them back on El Shaddai. Focus restored, he at last was able to let go of Benjamin and leave things up to God, giving proof to his new name, "Israel".

✔ Joseph's brothers were so racked with guilt and so shaken by the return of their money that they saw the money as a punishment from God and mistook Joseph's offer of hospitality for a prelude to revenge. But far from seeking revenge, Joseph was solicitous for his brothers' welfare and invited them to feast with him. He wept in longing for his younger brother and was guided by love and forgiveness in all that he did.

✔ The brothers' sin against Joseph was at root a sin against their father. Confident that his brothers repented of their sin against him, Joseph put his brothers to a final test to determine whether they loved their father. He planted a silver cup with Benjamin and sent his steward to charge him with theft. All the brothers returned with Benjamin to offer themselves as slaves to Joseph.

✔ Judah's eloquent plea to Joseph revealed a complete change of heart and a new depth of love for Jacob. Unwilling that his father should suffer, he offered himself as atonement for all his brothers.

✔ Joseph recognized that his family had been entirely healed of its deep wound caused by his brothers' lack of filial love. He finally revealed his identity, although his brothers were dismayed. Joseph put their minds at rest by saying that all they had done, however they meant it, was used by God to bring Joseph to Egypt and put him in a position to save lives. Even without an apology from them, Joseph forgave them. By doing this, he accomplished something far greater than retribution: the restoration of his family.

✔ In Joseph's emotional reunion with his brothers, the next step in God's plan for Jacob's family was revealed: they would move to Egypt, where Joseph had been sent in advance to prepare the way and provide for them.

For responses to Lesson 11 questions, see pp. 163-67.

Jacob's Family Moves to Egypt
(Genesis 46–50)

Joseph's emotional revelation of his identity to his brothers came at the end of his rigorous testing of them. Without knowing who he was, they had to prove that they were what they claimed to be—honest, true sons of one father. Their "three days" in the tomb of prison initiated a conversion in them. They understood and repented of their sin against Joseph. When faced with the opportunity to separate themselves from their youngest brother, Benjamin, who, at Joseph's hand, got them into a lot of trouble (just as in his youth Joseph's reports to Jacob of his brothers probably did), they chose solidarity instead. When Joseph insisted on enslaving only Benjamin, Judah offered his own life out of love for their father. At long last, Joseph's family was fully restored to him.

All that was left was to bring Jacob and all his brothers' families down to Egypt, to be near Joseph and to be safe from the famine. The relocation of Abraham's descendants, out of the land of Canaan, was a severe mercy. It saved them from dying of starvation, but it separated them from the Land of Promise. The food of Egypt filled their physical hunger, but did their departure from Canaan create an even deeper longing? What would happen when God's covenant people, the ones destined to bless all families on earth, found themselves in the most advanced, powerful nation in the world?

"He Opened to Us the Scriptures"

Before we read God's Word, we ought to take a moment to humble ourselves before Him, remembering that His Word is primarily a conversation with us, not a textbook. "Speak, Lord, for thy servant hears" (1 Sam. 3:9) can be the prayer on our lips. Because there are several Scripture passages to examine in this lesson, we suggest that you meditate on the following verse as you begin this study:

As for you, you meant evil against me; but God meant it for good, to bring it about that many people should be kept alive, as they are today.

—Gen. 50:20

Make a simple response to God and write your prayer in this space:

_____

_____

_____

_____

_____

Now, ask for His help as you work on the questions below.

❧

Questions
Israel Sets Out For Egypt

❧ **Read Genesis 46:1–7.**

1. As Jacob was leaving the land of Canaan to go down to Joseph in Egypt, God "spoke to Israel in visions of the night" (v. 2).

   a. When Jacob once before had left the land of Canaan for another place (for Haran, to flee Esau's wrath and find a wife), God also appeared to him in the night. Read Genesis 28:13–15. List the promises God made to Jacob there.

_____

_____

_____

_____

   b. Read Genesis 46:2–4. How was this night vision similar to the earlier one?

_____

_____

_____

_____

   c. *Challenge question*: Recall that God's appearance to Jacob at Bethel was Jacob's first personal encounter with the God of his fathers. This appearance to Jacob at Beersheba was His last. What does this last encounter between God and Jacob reveal about the fruit that the first encounter bore over the many years separating them?

_____

_____

_____

_____

Summary of Genesis 46:8–34

The author of Genesis takes the occasion of this move to Egypt to record a list of all the descendants of Israel (Jacob). Not long before, God's family was small: just Isaac and Rebecca, and Jacob, Rachel, and Leah. Now they are seventy, the number of completeness, suggesting a complete development in God's plan. To the Hebrews, seventy was the ideal and complete number: it was the number of descendants of Noah after the flood, corresponding in the ancient world to the seventy nations of the world; it was also the number of elders of Israel and of the disciples of Jesus. Why is this list here? This is the rootstock of the future nation of Israel.

Jacob's Family Settles in Goshen

❧ **Read Genesis 47:1–12.**

[*Note: Joseph settled his family in the region of Egypt called Goshen, a rich, fertile southern section of the country, located on the Nile River. It was "the best of the land" (v. 6), an indication of Joseph's very high standing in the court of Pharaoh.*]

2. Joseph brought Jacob in to see Pharaoh.

a. Why do you think Jacob blessed Pharaoh (v. 7)?

_____

_____

_____

_____

[*Note: Pharaoh inquired about Jacob's advanced age, possibly because the Hebrews lived longer than the Egyptians; Jacob would have seemed quite remarkable to them and would have been regarded as a great wise man.*]

b. *Challenge question*: When Jacob responded to Pharaoh's question about his age, he explained that his long years of life were "few and evil" compared to the longer lives of his ancestors, Abraham and Isaac. Why do you think he answered this way?

_____

_____

_____

_____

Summary of Genesis 47:13–26

The famine in Egypt was so severe that the Egyptians ran out of money to buy the grain they needed to survive. Joseph worked out an arrangement for them to give their animals in exchange for the grain. When they had gone through all their animals, they gave their land and even themselves to Pharaoh for the seed. Thus, it is no wonder that Pharaoh treated Joseph's family with such magnanimity when we consider that as a result of his program, Pharaoh owned everything in the land: all food, money, livestock, the land, and a fifth of what anyone produced on that land. (All with the exception of the land owned by the priests, whose food was allotted regularly by Pharaoh and who therefore had no need to sell their land.)

The people of Egypt sold everything to Pharaoh, including themselves, yet they also were helped in that their lives were saved from starvation. They did not become slaves in the way that Joseph had been a slave, but became what amounted to tenants of Pharaoh.

The nation of Egypt benefited from stability under Joseph's wise direction and may have enjoyed an increased influence among the neighboring countries, which had to come to her for food. All this was a tremendous boon for Israel. In addition to providing them with plenty of food, rich land to live in, and room to grow, Joseph's stable administration and Pharaoh's protection allowed them to grow in safety.

Jacob Prepares to Die

🕮 **Read Genesis 47:27–31.**

3. Israel and his family were "exceedingly" fruitful in their new home in Goshen, in spite of the great famine.

a. We know the famine lasted only seven years in Egypt (see Gen. 41:29–30). Why do you suppose Jacob and his family did not return to Canaan when the famine ended?

_____

_____

_____

_____

b. Why do you think Jacob made Joseph swear that he would bury his body back in the land of Canaan?

_____

_____

_____

_____

Jacob and Joseph's Sons
Read Genesis 48:1–32.

[*Note: As Jacob prepared to pass on the family blessing, he wanted to adopt Joseph's sons as his own, seemingly to replace any sons Rebekah might have had, had she lived longer. By saying, "Ephraim and Manasseh shall be mine, as Reuben and Simeon are" (v. 5), Jacob elevated them to the same level as his two oldest sons. Any future sons of Joseph would be counted under Ephraim and Manasseh in their inheritance.*]

4. Joseph brought his sons close to Jacob, whose eyesight was failing.

a. Look at what Jacob said to Joseph as he kissed the boys in verse 11. Read again the fears about his sons that once tortured Jacob in Genesis 42:36, 38. What replaced fear in Jacob's heart as he prepared to die? See also verses 15–16.

_____

_____

_____

_____

b. *Challenge question*: Joseph thought Jacob accidentally blessed the younger son ahead of the firstborn, but it was no accident. Jacob must have known from God that Joseph's younger son, Ephraim, was to receive the greater blessing. What is the deep irony in this scene?

_____

_____

_____

_____

"In Them Let My Name Be Perpetuated"

Jacob wanted his name to be perpetuated through Joseph's sons, Ephraim and Manasseh. History bore out this desire. When the sons of Jacob returned to Canaan, Manasseh's allotment of land included the plot of land Jacob gave to Joseph (see v. 22). Later in their history, the kingdom of David was divided in two, Israel (the Northern Kingdom) and Judah (the Southern Kingdom). Israel was often called "Ephraim" by the Hebrews. Thus Jacob's name lived on in his grandson.

After Jacob adopted Ephraim and Manasseh and blessed Joseph through them, he had in effect thirteen sons who would father the tribes of Israel. The tribes were officially numbered at twelve, which corresponds with the original number of Jacob's sons, because Levi's tribe was spread among the others and not given its own territory.

c. What assurance did Jacob want to give Joseph as he lay dying (v. 21)?

_____

_____

_____

_____

d. *Challenge question*: Jacob gave one "portion" or "mountain slope" to Joseph that none of his brothers received (v. 22). This was probably a reference to the land of Shechem (see Josh. 24:32). Why do you think he did that?

_____

_____

_____

_____

Summary of Genesis 49:1–27

After blessing Joseph, Jacob called his other sons together to bless them, or as he said, to tell "what shall befall you in days to come" (v. 1). The blessing foretold the futures of the tribes that would bear their names. History confirmed the predictions. It is worth noting some of them here:

Reuben would lose the preeminence due to him naturally as the firstborn, because he slept with Bilhah, his father's concubine (Gen. 35:22). This was tantamount to an attempt to claim his father's authority and position for himself.

Simeon and Levi, cursed for their violence, would be divided and scattered: Simeon eventually was absorbed into Judah, and Levi was dispersed among the other tribes as priests.

Judah, the fourth son who had been willing to ransom all his brothers' freedom with his own, was given pride of place. His tribe would rule over those of his brothers. It would be prosperous and strong, described with the imagery of a lion cub. Most importantly, Jacob foretold that "the scepter shall not depart from Judah . . . until he comes to whom it belongs" (v. 10). The initial fulfillment of this prophecy came in the kingdom and dynasty God established in David. Beyond that, "he . . . to whom it belongs" was traditionally believed by the Jews to point to the Messiah. Jesus, the "Lion of the tribe of Judah," reigns in righteousness and justice on David's throne forever.

Joseph received a further blessing here, and it is hard to miss how much in length and tone it stands out from the others. Jacob's repetition of "bless" and "blessing" (six times in verses 25 and 26 alone) impart a deep sense of God's blessing. The passage gives the effect of richness, of blessing "pressed down, shaken together and running over" (Lk. 6:38). Because we know the story of Joseph's life, we are not confused by this kind of "favoritism" by a father for his son. We understand that the son, who was unusually blessed and favored, used those graces to serve and save his family and the world. A "beloved son" like this stirs up not jealousy but gratitude.

Jacob Breathed His Last

⚜ **Read Genesis 49:28–50:3.**

5. Jacob made a deathbed request (Gen. 49:29–32).

   a. What was on his mind and heart as he closed his eyes in death?

_____

_____

_____

_____

   b. Why do you think he made this request of his children?

_____

_____

_____

_____

Summary of Genesis 50:4–14

Joseph requested and received permission from Pharaoh to take his father's body to the land of Canaan for burial. All of Jacob's family and a very large entourage of Egyptians made the journey with him to the cave Abraham had bought for Sarah's body, in the field of Machpela, east of Mamre. The burial party made "a very great and sorrowful lamentation" (v. 10) for Jacob. The Canaanites who saw it remarked, "This is a grievous mourning to the Egyptians" (v. 11). Thus was Jacob's wish to be buried in Canaan fulfilled. Then all his family returned to Egypt.

Joseph and His Brothers

⚜ **Read Genesis 50:15–21.**

6. After their father's death, Joseph's brothers feared that he would take revenge on them for their sin against him.

   a. Why do you suppose that their father's death raised this fear in them again?

_____

_____

_____

_____

b. What did their fear prompt them to do that they had never done before (vv. 17–18)?

_____

_____

_____

_____

c. Why do you think Joseph wept over this?

_____

_____

_____

_____

d. In their fear, what had they forgotten about their sin, of which Joseph had to remind them (v. 20)?

_____

_____

_____

_____

Joseph Dies

🕮 **Read Genesis 50:22–26.**

7. As Joseph faced death, his abiding desire was to be returned to the land of Canaan, just as Jacob's had been.

a. *Challenge question*: In the Epistle to the Hebrews, Saint Paul (its probable author) wrote about Abraham and his descendants. Read Hebrews 11:17–22. Abraham, Isaac, Jacob, and Joseph all lived "by faith." How would you define faith from what Saint Paul says about these men? See also Hebrews 11:1–2.

_____

_____

_____

_____

b. *Challenge question*: Approaching death caused both Jacob and Joseph to long for home, for the land of Canaan. Their family life as God's covenant people had been fully healed. God had kept every promise to them. All that was left was a return to the land God had given to Abraham.

For a Christian, imminent death can also produce a longing. What does a Christian long for when he contemplates death? See the *Catechism*, nos. 1010–11.

_____

_____

_____

_____

In the End Is the Beginning

With chapter 50 comes the end of "The Beginning," the end of the book of Genesis. What began in Eden, with the gift of life altered tragically by death, ends with the death of the man who prefigures the One through whom that life would be restored. The record of the death of Joseph not only closes the era of the patriarchs, it also points forward to things yet to come.

This final chapter showed Joseph's strong faith that God would fulfill His promises. Half a century passed without mention as the embryonic nation grew in the womb of Egypt. The final words of the book, "and he was put in a coffin in Egypt," may close the page on Joseph, but they beckon us to look forward to the rest of the story. That story is recorded in the Book of Exodus, which begins with the news that as the Israelites multiplied and filled the land, a new king came to power and enslaved them, making their lives bitter. It is not too far-fetched to imagine that Joseph's coffin, left waiting to be returned to his fathers, stood as a constant reminder to Israel to have faith in the God who promises the impossible . . . and does what He promises.

※

"Did Not Our Hearts Burn Within Us?"

Our hearts will burn with joy when we consciously open them wide to God's Word. Scripture memorization is a good way to get that started. Here is a suggested memory verse:

As for you, you meant evil against me; but God meant it for good, to bring it about that many people should be kept alive, as they are today.

—Gen. 50:20

Continue to welcome Him into your soul by reflecting on these questions:

Jacob's story is an amazing chronicle of a man who was born into the covenant of his people with God but who experienced a true conversion as an adult. Over the long course of his life, as a result of his response to God's visitation in a dream, Jacob lived increasingly in the warmth of God's love. His life was not without difficulties, but his sufferings deepened their relationship. He died a humble, grateful "servant of God," as his sons called him. He closed his eyes in the sleep of death in the presence of his beloved Joseph, an unspeakably loving gift from God.

Jacob helps us to recognize that the longer we walk with God, the more we should experience the tenderness and peace that comes from intimacy with Him. Now would be a good time to check your own relationship with God, to see if it is bearing the fruit of a personal encounter with Him. Does He call you by name? Does He comfort you when you are afraid? Does He help you go on when you're sure you can't? Is your heart full of awe and gratitude, like Jacob's was, over all the wonderful things He has done for you? This is life with God; is it your life?

_____

_____

_____

_____

_____

Jacob and Joseph did not want their family to forget that Egypt wasn't their true home. Likewise, Jesus did not want His followers to mistakenly settle too comfortably in this world, because it is not our true home; heaven is. We are to have that same longing for and determination to reach home that Israel had while they were in Egypt.

How can we tell if we've forgotten where we're headed? If we find ourselves stockpiling possessions, fretting over finances, or trying to squeeze perfect happiness out of our spouses, our children, our jobs, etc., then we may need to remember that we are only passing through this world. Is this a reminder you could use now?

_____

_____

_____

_____

_____

"Stay with Us"

Our study of the patriarchs of Genesis began with God's call to one man, Abraham. The call was for Abraham to leave home for a new life, and included in the call were abundant promises of blessing. The proliferation of blessings in God's promises to Abraham signaled to us that God had begun His work of restoring what had been lost in the original Land of Promise, which was Eden. God's plan was to create a family, then a nation from that family, to be His very own and to return blessing to the whole earth. The plan got underway with the miracle birth of a baby boy to Abraham and Sarah. The plan also included testing and purification. Above all, the plan was human and personal. What a surprise! After Eden, we would have expected God to avoid using human beings to advance His work in the world. There they proved themselves weak and unreliable.

As we have followed the story of Abraham's family, we have had to cringe more than once over God's choice of these people to restore humanity to Himself. Yet the pattern of God's plan has been clear right from the start: the sinful human beings joined to Him in a covenant underwent a transformation. No matter how weak and feeble they were at the beginning of their lives with God, at the end their faith in Him was confident and strong. Think of Abraham on top of Mount Moriah, giving to all generations after him a living picture of God's willingness to give His own Son as a sacrifice for us. Think of Jacob, who began his covenant life as a schemer and manipulator, but who ended his days full of rapturous awe and gratitude to God, blessed by Him and a blessing to others. Think of Jacob's sons, who fathered the twelve tribes that became the nation of Israel. They were an unsteady and scary lot! Yet in the end, they also were new men—reconciled to their father and each other in a most remarkable way.

Human transformation in covenant life has been a consistent theme in our study of the patriarchs. Yet human transformation was not the whole story of God's plan for Redemption. The other abiding reality of how God works in the world has been the appearance of miraculous humans to initiate and advance God's plan. Isaac, the long-awaited son of Abraham and Sarah, was a miracle baby, "the child of promise," as Saint Paul called him (cf. Gal. 4:28). The nation of Israel, with all its future blessings, could not have existed without his birth. The advanced age of his parents, as well as the barrenness of his mother, proved beyond any doubt that he existed through the gracious, miraculous intervention of God.

Among the sons of Jacob, it was Joseph who was the miraculous human being. Full of virtue, gifted with extraordinary dreams and the ability to interpret them, preserved and blessed by God in the most trying circumstances, Joseph's graced life was a beacon of light among the descendants of Abraham. Even more than Isaac, Joseph helps us to understand that God's plan to bless the world includes His gifts to the world, in human flesh. The stories of the patriarchs teach us that the return to Eden will be a work both human and divine. The initiative will always be God's; it does not depend on humans. However, humans are drawn up into it in a most exquisite way. Redemption will always have a human face.

How satisfyingly appropriate this great truth is! It plants our feet firmly in the Paradise that was lost through human sin: "Let us make man in our image, after our likeness" (Gen. 1:26).

All is not lost after all.

Lesson Summary

✔ God confirmed His promise to Jacob one last time as he left for Egypt. In doing so, He reassured Jacob that this move was part of His plan: He would prepare Jacob's family in Egypt to become a nation, and He would be with them and bring them back to Canaan.

✔ A list of Jacob's descendants who settled in Egypt suggested a complete development in this stage of God's plan: the rootstock of the future nation of Israel had been planted.

✔ By presenting his family to Pharaoh as shepherds, a class of people who were "detestable to the Egyptians," Joseph was able to obtain for them the land of Goshen: a fertile area where they could prosper, separating from the Egyptians so they could grow as a people under God. In Egypt they enjoyed the protection of Pharaoh, the provision of Joseph, and the blessing of God.

✔ The same famine that reduced the Egyptians to vassals of Pharaoh served to enrich Israel—clear evidence of God's care and blessing. Joseph's administrative policies were beneficial to everyone: they prospered Pharaoh, stabilized Egypt, saved the people from death, and strengthened Israel. Clearly, God's Spirit guided Joseph to extend His blessing to the entire world.

✔ In preparing to die, Jacob turned his thoughts toward God. His final words of blessing were filled with faith that God would do as He has said.

✔ In a final blessing, Jacob bypassed his older sons in favor of the sons of Joseph and assigned royal leadership among the tribes to Judah. His words pointed forward to the Messiah who would come from that tribe to rule an everlasting kingdom and who later would be called "Lion of the Tribe of Judah."

✔ Jacob's final request to be buried in Canaan revealed that his heart was at home with his fathers and showed his faith that God would one day bring his family out of Egypt. Joseph's last words echoed those of Jacob: although he was about to die, the others could be assured that God would take them home.

✔ Genesis concluded with a forward look in hope for God's salvation, even as it began with the story of man's fall and his need for that salvation.

For responses to Lesson 12 questions, turn to pp. 167-71.

Appendix

Guide to Lesson Questions

Lesson 1

To make the most of this study, respond to all the questions yourself before reading these responses.

God Calls Abram (Gen. 12:1–3)

1. a. God told Abram to leave everything and go to a place unknown to him. He had to make a clean break with what was familiar and dear to him.

b. Responses will vary. God had made Abram a wonderful promise, but in order to receive it, he had to go out from his old way of life and trust God to make a new home for him. He was about to start an entirely new life, away from all the customs and religious practices of his father's house. This action by Abram, in which God asked him to step out and embrace the gift He wanted to give him, is the first glimpse we have in Scripture of what *conversion* looks like. To follow Jesus always means to leave something behind in order to receive the kingdom of God.

2. *Challenge question*: We know that in Eden, God blessed man because he was pleasing in His sight. That blessing was later replaced by a curse, as man fell from grace and from favor in God's eyes. Likewise, when Noah left the ark and built an altar to the Lord, the smell of the sacrifice pleased God, and He blessed Noah and his family. Before too long, however, there was also a curse put on part of Noah's family. Here in these verses there is such an explosion of blessing that we can only draw one conclusion: God intended to use Abram and his descendants to restore His blessing on all mankind. The blessing on Abram would be so far reaching that generations yet unborn would experience it.

It would take centuries for all the details to get worked out, but there is no missing the fact that God wanted to restore humanity to its original blessedness. He had a plan to do it that involved a nation with a unique relationship with Him. Somehow this nation would provide an open door for all men everywhere to be blessed. This promise to Abram was not just about a new place to live. It was a promise that would regain Paradise, for him and all who came after him.

3. Yes, it was risky for God to associate His plan so closely with humans. We have already seen examples of human weakness, and we expect to see many more. Yet God has shown Himself willing to take risks in order to do things the way He intends. His daring use of the rainbow as a sign of the covenant with Noah showed that He wanted to preserve humanity as He created it, alive in both body (the senses) and soul. His promise to bless men through the mediation of human flesh was even more outrageous. Yet it was simply a development of the promise God made in the Garden to defeat His enemy *through* human beings. The work of God to win the world back to Himself will always have a human face on it. God's promise to Abram is another occasion for us to marvel afresh over the love of God for creatures made of dust like us.

Abram Sets Out (Gen. 12:4–9)

4. Abram was willing to leave his earthly security and whatever power was his as Terah's firstborn son to obey the voice of God (whom he barely knew). He set out for a land he'd never seen and knew nothing about. In other words, his trust in God put him in a position of complete dependence. That dependency is a sharp contrast to the builders of Babel. They refused to be scattered over the earth, choosing instead to consolidate their technology and power. Their intention to make a name for themselves and to build a tower to heaven showed them to be unwilling to live in humility, without knowing what comes next. The irony is that Abram, who was willing to leave behind his comfortable place on earth in order to obey God, received a promise of unthinkable power and influence. He was to become the father of a great nation, Israel. It would be a descendant of his, Jesus, who would bring heaven to earth in the Incarnation (no need for a tower!). Abram lost everything to obey; in obeying, he gained *more* than everything in return.

5. Responses will vary. We don't know for sure why Abram took Lot with him. Since Abram and Sarai were without children, perhaps they had formed a close bond with their nephew, whose father, Haran, was already dead. Perhaps Lot had an adventurous spirit and begged to go along on the journey. Perhaps Abram wanted someone in his household who would remind him of home. Whatever the reason, although God's call to Abram didn't mention him, Lot joined the sojourners on the trip to the land of Canaan.

6. Abram developed great reverence for God. He must have been thankful for God's presence with him in the strange land; he must have felt wonder in knowing that God intended to give him the land that lay before him. He was learning to worship the one, true God in his new life, in the same way that his forefather, Seth, had done.

Abram Is Tested (Gen. 12:10–20)

7. a. Abram must have had wonderful expectations about what God was about to do for him. Although it must have been difficult to leave the known for the unknown, the promise of God to abundantly bless him surely gave Abram some confidence

that it would all work out. A famine would have put that confidence to the test. He may have experienced disturbing doubts: "What am I doing here? Why did I ever leave the security of my father's house? If I had stayed there, I probably wouldn't be facing starvation."

b. He responded by going down to Egypt, where he expected food to be more plentiful. This was not necessarily a bad thing in itself. In fact, the history of Israel would later be characterized by two other flights into Egypt for safety—one by the brothers of Joseph and their families when they were faced with famine. The other was the flight of another Joseph, the husband of Mary, when he took his family there to escape Herod's murderous rage against the newborn King of Israel.

c. Responses will vary. Perhaps Abram should have asked God what he should do about the famine. This would have been an opportunity for him to learn to trust God in a difficult, unexpected situation.

8. a. Abram feared for his life, so he urged Sarai to cooperate in a deception of the Pharaoh. This was certainly wrong of him to do. Even the Pharaoh recognized that.

b. God prevented further damage by afflicting Pharaoh's household with plagues making sexual contact between Sarah and anyone there unlikely (the judgment of God is always a sign of His *mercy*). God did what was necessary to convince Abram to live righteously. He showed great patience with Abram's weakness. He understood the fear that prompted the sin and so set Abram back on the path to restoration. In this crisis, God also taught Abram an important lesson. For Abram to see God at work in Egypt, following him wherever he went, would have shown him that this God was not like pagan deities, who were associated with specific locations. This God was *everywhere*.

c. God did not want to start over with someone more reliable; He wanted to make Abram into a more reliable man. Would Abram cooperate with God? This was the question God had put to Cain: "If you do well, will you not be accepted?" (Gen. 4:7). It is the question He asks each one of us. He shows Himself willing to work with us in our weakness; it is rebellion and turning away from Him that will exclude Him from our lives.

9. *Challenge question*: Responses will vary. This is a question that is good to raise, but it is not possible to fully answer now. We will need to see more of God's work unfold before we can say for sure. The simplest answer in the meantime is a common proverb: there is strength in numbers. We have seen in Genesis that righteousness in man after the Fall, where it could be found, was fragile. It was easily overwhelmed or diluted by weakness or by contact with men who rebel against authority and give themselves over to pride. A righteous life is difficult to live in isolation. God desired to build a strong human community in order to strengthen His people to resist evil.

There is another reason why God chose one nation in this way. If God created an entire nation for Himself, it would be a nation with a religion that reflected the truth about what He wanted men to know about Him and how they should worship Him. Its laws would reflect how He wanted men to live with each other. A nation like that could act as an example of righteousness to the others and thus become a deterrent to evil. If the people of this nation were strictly prohibited from intermarriage with other cultures (as they were in Israel), there would be a hope of preserving the truth from corruption. To create a nation for Himself was God's strategy to save the whole world.

Lesson 2

To make the most of this study, respond to all the questions yourself before reading these responses.

Abram Returns to Canaan (Gen. 13:1–13)

1. a. Abram returned to the first altar he had built in the land of Canaan, and he "called on the name of the Lord" (Gen. 13:4).

b. Abram's return to the first altar he had built, at Bethel, and his calling on the name of the Lord suggest that he desired to make a fresh start in the life with God he had begun. Because of the plagues on Pharaoh's household, surely he was aware that the Lord was displeased with his behavior in Egypt. He perhaps felt the need to demonstrate that he wanted to live in a way that brought honor to God's name. It was a beautiful picture of the appropriate response of men when they stumble into sin. Unlike Cain, who let his sin turn into wholesale rebellion against God (Gen. 4:6–8), Abram returned and did what was right.

2. a. Abram's large herds meant that he and Lot could not dwell together on the land in Canaan. This created strife in the family, which led to a separation. It is worth taking note that this first mention of great wealth in the Scripture is associated with unhappiness and lack of peace. This will become a frequent theme in the rest of Scripture. Of course, wealth in and of itself is not the source of trouble. Rather, it is man's inclination to become so attached to it that can bring such misery. This seems not to have happened in Abram, however. His great wealth did later enable him to put together an army when it was necessary to lead a rescue mission under dangerous circumstances. Yet, as we will see, Abram's heart was not entangled in his possessions. He appears to have been the kind of man whose treasures were not of this world, the kind of man Jesus would one day describe as one who lays up treasures in heaven, where there can be no threat to peace or happiness (see Mt. 6:19–21).

b. Abram seemed to strongly desire peace in his family. He generously offered Lot the first choice of the land. Being the head of the family and Lot's elder, he could rightfully have laid claim to the first choice and best of the land. He seemed to prize peace more than good land. He was not a selfish man.

3. *Challenge question*: Responses will vary. Lot's eyes told him to choose the land that looked like paradise (v. 10). He wanted for himself the land that appeared to be the absolute best. We might well wonder why Lot didn't show any deference to his uncle, even out of politeness. He could have said, "No, Uncle, you make the first choice. That would only be right." Perhaps he wanted to avoid facing another famine in Canaan. The text tells us that the valley that looked so beautiful to Lot was the home of Sodom, a city of great wickedness. The language here is reminiscent of a scene in the Garden of Eden, when Eve sized up the forbidden fruit (see Gen. 3:6). Looks can be deceiving.

The Lord Renews His Promise (Gen. 13:14–18)

4. a. If Abram's descendants were ever to become a "great nation," as God had promised, the first thing they would need was *land*. Tribes of people without land of their own remain just that—tribes of people. God told Abram to take a good look at the land itself. This was the concrete reality that lay before his eyes. The land was real to him; the promise of descendants to fill it was still a hope, which depended entirely on God's trustworthiness. This is reminiscent of God's use of the rainbow with Noah. With the rainbow and with the land of Canaan, God used a concrete reality within nature as a sign of His promise to act. In the Church, God continues to do this in the sacraments.

b. Responses will vary. Abram may have been thinking the same kind of thoughts we think when we approach a sacrament. "All I see here is land—dirt, rocks, bushes. God says this will be the home of my great nation. I don't have any kids, and my wife is barren. Can I really believe this?" In the sacraments, we are always faced with these very human questions. "This is just water on a baby's head. Is this child *really* being washed from original sin and given the Holy Spirit?" "This looks and tastes like bread and wine. Can I *really* believe that I am eating the Body and Blood of the Lord and that it will give me eternal life?" When we think those thoughts, we are much like Abram, walking through that desert land, pondering the promises of God. That is why his response will be of interest to us.

5. a. Abram built an altar to the Lord at Hebron. It was an act of reverence, worship, and faith. He must have mulled over God's promise to him and come to the conclusion that God was worthy to be worshiped this way. Building an altar was his acknowledgment of trust in the promises of God.

b. *Challenge question*: The verses in Hebrews tell us that faith is "the assurance of things hoped for, the conviction of things not seen." Picture Abram walking through the land of Canaan, observing all its physical characteristics and trying to imagine his descendants living there as a great nation. When he built an altar to the Lord, he gave evidence of a trust in unseen realities. He performed an act of confidence in God, believing that He would do what He had promised. This is the essence of faith. It is like what Noah did when he built an ark on dry ground. It acknowledged that God, who cannot be seen, could nevertheless be trusted completely. The sacraments call forth just such faith. When we exercise that faith, we are standing with Abram, the father of faith, believing that what we can see confirms what we can't.

Abram Goes to Battle (Gen. 14:1–16)

6. a. Abram had earlier showed himself to be a man dedicated to his family. He showed by his rescue of Lot that this love had not diminished and that it was a fearless love. He demonstrated courage and ingenuity in defeating the enemy.

b. Responses will vary. Remember, when Abram sojourned in Egypt, he had a problem with lack of courage. Because of the intensity of the battles that had raged, he might easily have talked himself out of such a risky operation. In addition, he could have justifiably left Lot to live with the consequences of choosing to live in Sodom, a wicked city. His decision to go immediately to Lot's rescue, whatever the cost, revealed him to be strong and free in his love for his nephew. He was willing and able to do what was right.

Abram's Victory (Gen. 14:17–24)

7. a. Abram did not want to be indebted to the king of Sodom. That kind of debt could have presented problems for him in a variety of ways, so he turned down the offer for great personal gain.

b. *Challenge question*: Responses will vary. Because Abram had an answer ready for the king of Sodom, when the offer for gain was presented, it was possible that when he first learned of Lot's predicament, he spoke to God about it all. Perhaps he asked for God's help in making the rescue. Perhaps he had to face down fears over losing his life in battle. Melchizedek's blessing on Abram suggests that God answered this prayer ("blessed be God Most High, who has delivered your enemies into your hands"). Is it possible that God warned him to stand firm in the face of temptation to be drawn under the influence of the king of Sodom? Abram understood very well that he would have to appear to be coming to the rescue of the wicked as well as the good when he rescued Lot. Yet his solemn vow to God in verse 22 ("I have sworn to the LORD God Most High") shows that he was able to distinguish one from the other and to maintain his proper allegiance. This is reminiscent of the temptation the devil laid before Jesus in the desert: "Again, the devil took him to a very high mountain, and showed him all the kingdoms of the world and the glory of them; and he said to him, 'All these I will give you, if you will fall down and worship me.' Then Jesus said to him, 'Begone, Satan! for it is written, 'You shall worship the Lord your God and him only shall you serve.' Then the devil left him" (Mt. 4:8–11).

8. These three men, recipients of Abram's generosity, would perhaps be more likely to remain his allies, respecting him as a just man. Considering the hostilities that raged in the land, Abram would have been wise to consolidate this kind of alliance. In this, Abram was an example of what Jesus, many years later, would teach His followers: "Behold, I send you out as sheep in the midst of wolves; so be wise as serpents and innocent as doves" (Mt. 10:16).

9. Responses will vary. Abram was an example of a "just" man; that is, he gave both God and men their due. In his dealings with men, he was devoted to his family, willing to act in a generously unselfish way in order to settle a dispute that threatened peace. This family solidarity led him to act courageously to rescue Lot, doing whatever it took to free him from harm. Outside the family, he acted wisely in his dealings with men, knowing when to remain detached from them and when to seal alliances.

In his dealings with God, Abram was a man who had humility. He turned toward God, not away, when he stumbled. As he contemplated the almost unthinkable promise that God had made to him, he performed an act of reverence and faith. When Abram was met by Melchizedek, the priest of God Most High, he received a blessing from him, a sign of finding favor in God's sight. Abram's response of giving the priest a tenth of everything showed him to be someone who was beginning to deeply comprehend that if God is "maker of heaven and earth," as Melchizedek called Him (Gen. 14:19), then He is worthy of generous offerings. Perhaps this was why he was able to be detached from the temptation to become indebted to the king of a wicked city, declaring a vow of allegiance to God.

Abram is coming into focus as a man we can respect. He learns from his mistakes, has a deep reverence for God, acts courageously for the sake of love, acts wisely and unselfishly for the sake of peace, and recognizes that God is supreme over all and worthy of undivided loyalty.

Lesson 3

To make the most of this study, respond to all the questions yourself before reading these responses.

Abram Questions God (Gen. 15:1–6)

1. Perhaps the reality of what Abram had done in spurning the king of Sodom's offer began to sink in, causing him some concern. He had been heroic in giving a tithe of all he owned, and he had stood firm in the face of temptation by a powerful king. Yet what would be the practical effects of those noble choices? Would he become an enemy to this king? Would his alliances with the other three men hold up, or would he be left vulnerable to intrigue and attack? He had given up some of his wealth and turned down the possibility of more, but what if circumstances in the region changed? What if there was another famine? What if, what if . . . It is not surprising, then, that God appeared to Abram to confirm and encourage him in his choices. "Fear not," God told him, and He promised to be Abram's defender. As for his loss of money and possibly his security in the land, whatever he lost would be made up in a "great reward." This visit from God showed that He was well aware of the ebbs and flows of faith, that creatures made of dust need reassurance from time to time, even (or perhaps especially) after they have made a heroic act of faith.

2. a. Abram suggested that God had not kept His promise of giving him an heir.

b. Responses will vary. Abram's mind had been fixed on this dilemma long enough for him to think he had to come up with another plan to obtain an heir. Eliezer was Abram's slave; it was not uncommon in that culture for barren couples to adopt a son to make him their heir. Abram thought that he would have to resort to this practice because God had not given him a son of his own. We can't miss the tone of disappointment and frustration in his words. The long wait for Abram and Sarai to see concrete proof of God's promise was taking its toll.

3. a. The first thing God did in response to Abram's doubt was to speak the truth to him: "Your own son shall be your heir." Perhaps Abram thought that he had misunderstood God—there had been no mention *directly* of his own son being his heir, although that was certainly the implication. God spoke to clear away Abram's second-guessing.

b. Responses will vary. Abram was probably hoping that God would give him a timetable of when this son would appear. Maybe he hoped that God would acknowledge that he and Sarai weren't getting any younger; perhaps he hoped to hear God say, "It's time to get on with this." That is not what happened. Instead, God directed Abram's attention to a beautiful sight in nature, the countless stars of heaven. He did not defend or explain Himself to Abram. He simply joined His own word of promise to the witness of the night sky to answer Abram's doubts. Then He left the decision up to Abram; he would have to decide whether what he could see in the stars would enable him to trust God for the son he couldn't yet see.

4. Responses will vary. Perhaps when God first took Abram outside to look at the stars, he was disappointed. So many questions must have been racing through his head: "How long will I have to wait to see this son that has been promised to me? Ten years is a long time! Did I make a big mistake in leaving my father's house to come out here to this strange land? Who is this God, anyway? What will I tell Sarai? Will she really believe that she's going to become pregnant with my son? And now I'm told to look at the stars. How's that going to help?" Maybe those questions kept him distracted for a time, looking at the stars but not really seeing them.

Yet think about what a starry night looks like. We know that what Abram saw was more magnificent than any night we've seen, since all of us live in the modern era of artificial light and an atmosphere affected by pollution. Even modern men, however, stand in awe of the wonder of the heavens at night. What do the stars inspire? They make us feel small enough to be humble, which is always a good thing. The sheer vastness of the sky and the countless lights of the stars make us marvel over the creation and its Creator. The stars give us a respect for God's power. Paradoxically, they also move us to amazement that in a universe of such size, God knows and cares about us, about me. While stargazing, most of us eventually become very quiet in the presence of this great mystery. If we spend time looking at the night sky, words start to seem like an intrusion. We simply want to drink it all in, which only silence seems to accommodate properly.

Is this what happened to Abram? Was his face at first creased with doubt and frustration? Was it a mirror of all the years, months, days, and minutes that went into those ten years of waiting? Were his eyes in one place but his mind another? God left him in silence to take a good, long look. Was Abram gradually caught up in the reverie that the night sky always creates? Did his face begin to relax, his dazzled eyes to shine with wonder? How long did he look at that sky? We don't know what time it was when God took him out there. Did Abram lie down on the ground, to mull it all over? We know that the action that follows in verses 7–11 happened during the day. That means Abram might have looked at the stars *all night*. We don't know how much time lapsed between God's statement in verse 5 and Abram's act of faith in verse 6. Quite possibly it took him many hours, even until dawn, to make his decision to put his doubts aside and believe the Lord.

It seems his doubts were finally silenced by the wordless testimony of the star-filled sky: "The heavens are telling the glory of God; and the firmament proclaims his handiwork. Day to day pours forth speech, and night to night declares knowledge. There is no speech, nor are there words, their voice is not heard; yet their voice goes out through all the earth, and their words to the end of the world" (Ps. 19:1–4). Abram "heard" the "voice" that "is not heard" and put his confidence in God.

5. Responses will vary. When Abram left his home in Haran, trusting in the promises of God, everything lay ahead of him. He barely knew anything about God; surely he was filled with excited expectation. When he had lived in the land for ten years without receiving the promised son, he had lived with the reality that sometimes God can disappoint, confuse, bewilder, and exasperate us. For a man to consciously choose to continue to believe in God, in the teeth of this reality, shows an extraordinary trust in God's character. It is a faith that says, "Not my will but Yours."

6. Responses will vary. In this very first prayer recorded in the Bible, several characteristics are worth remembering:

- It was God drawing near to Abram that drew forth a prayer from him. As the *Catechism* says, "In prayer, the faithful God's initiative of love always comes first; our own first step is always a response. As God gradually reveals himself and reveals man to himself, prayer appears as a reciprocal call, a covenant drama" (no. 2567).
- Abram was honest with God. He poured out his anxieties and doubts. He was not afraid to say what he thought.
- Abram not only spoke to God, but he also listened to Him as well. There was a word of truth from God that he must hear, even though he had many of his own thoughts and words.
- Abram spent some time in silence, looking at the stars and considering God's promise. The silent pondering of the stars may have looked like nothing was happening, yet it was the occasion of Abram's movement from doubt to faith.
- Abram performed an act of faith. He consciously set aside his doubts and put his trust in God, which made him pleasing to God.

In summary, we see that Abram's prayer was a response to God's love. It was honest and intimate. It was a conversation, with speaking and listening. It included silence, and it led to a conscious act of faith.

God's Covenant with Abram (Gen. 15:7–21)

7. *Challenge question*: Abram had already put his trust in God, so the question he asked cannot have been prompted by doubt. Perhaps he was asking for some physical demonstration that would give evidence of the promise God made for the land, just as the stars had been evidence of his human descendants. It was not the question, "What will You show me that will make me believe?" Rather, it was the question, "What will You show me that represents the promise You have made?" He was asking for a sign of the covenant God was making with him, not for a sign of God's trustworthiness. The joining of God's promises to material realities in nature has always been at the heart of God's covenants with men.

8. a. It looks like Abram once again had to wait on God. If he had to chase away the birds of prey, the carcasses must have been lying there for a while.

b. Responses will vary. There must have been time for doubts to creep into Abram's mind. Did he have to fend them off, just as he fended off the birds? Did he wonder when God was going to show up and make something meaningful out of this scene of death?

  This picture of Abram, sitting in the sun with a pile of dead animals, waiting for God to act, is a powerful one. In a way, it will be repeated throughout the history of Israel and the history of man. Israel, the great nation promised to Abram, would repeatedly lie in pieces, waiting on God to act. The Church, the new Israel, continues this waiting. "Though already present in his Church, Christ's reign is nevertheless yet to be fulfilled 'with power and great glory' by the king's return to earth [Lk. 21:27; cf. Mt. 25:31]. This reign is still under attack by the evil powers, even though they have been defeated definitively by Christ's Passover [cf. 2 Thess. 2:7]. Until everything is subject to him, 'until there be realized new heavens and a new earth in which justice dwells, the pilgrim Church, in her sacraments and institutions, which belong to this present age, carries the mark of this world which will pass, and she herself takes her place among the creatures which groan and travail yet and await the revelation of the sons of God' [*LG* 48 § 3; cf. 2 Pet. 3:13; Rom. 8:19–22; 1 Cor. 15:28]. That is why Christians pray, above all in the Eucharist, to hasten Christ's return by saying to him [cf. 1 Cor. 11:26; 2 Pet. 3:11–12]: *Marana tha*! 'Our Lord, come!' [1 Cor. 16:22; Rev. 22:17, 20]" (*Catechism*, no. 671).

9. *Challenge question*: Abram's deep sleep is reminiscent of Adam's sleep, when God solved the only problem he had in Eden, which was being alone. It perhaps represents man's ultimate inability to solve his own problems or ensure his own fate. It underscores dramatically how divine initiative and human helplessness come together to accomplish God's loving purposes (think of the sleeping apostles in the Garden of Gethsemane, upon whom Christ intended to build His Church).

10. Responses will vary. The fate of the nation that would come from Abram suggests that it would be a nation that understood a very important lesson: God chose Israel not because it was a better nation than all the others—how can a nation of slaves in bondage have anything to boast about? He chose them because He wanted to show His power to those who, humanly speaking, have no hope of saving themselves. In their own national history, they would live out the story of Eden, a story of human beings in bondage and very far from home, whose only hope is the power and mercy of God. The greatness of Israel was meant to be rooted in humility.

11. *Challenge question*: Responses will vary. Fire has the amazing characteristic of producing opposite effects in those who experience it. Its light can lead the way or make us draw back. Its appearance can console or terrify. Its heat can sustain or destroy; it can harden or melt. How the fire is experienced depends on what comes into contact with it. In that sense, fire is an apt symbol of God's presence. It does justice to all that He is in His essence. The Scripture consistently refers to the fire of God, as both an expression of His power and love, as well as His wrath and judgment.

Lesson 4

To make the most of this study, respond to all the questions yourself before reading these responses.

Sarai's Plan (Gen. 16:1–6)

1. **a.** Abram blurted his doubts out to God. He struggled to believe that God would come through with a son, but he was not afraid to lay his doubts out before God, asking, "What wilt thou give me?" (Gen. 15:2). He even made a veiled charge against God for not keeping His Word: "Behold, thou hast given me no offspring" (Gen. 15:3). His mind raced ahead to come up with another plan, in case the first one had to be scratched.

   Sarai's doubts were very similar to Abram's. She, too, wanted to hold God responsible for her lack of a son: "[T]he LORD has prevented me from bearing children" (Gen. 16:2). This is a little stronger accusation than Abram's. His was a charge of failure to act; hers was a charge of meddlesome intervention. Her mind also raced ahead to come up with an alternative plan of action. The big difference between how they each doubted is that Abram spoke his doubts to God; Sarai seems to have let them burn inside of her. Abram questioned God; Sarai issued orders.

   b. Responses will vary. Perhaps we want to excuse Sarai by saying that it was Abram who had the intimate relationship with God, not her. He was the head of the home and acted as the priest of the family. How would she have an opportunity to speak her doubts to God? She could have presented her doubts to Abram, with a simple request: "Ask God about it." Instead, she took things into her own hands. She circumvented both Abram and God.

2. **a.** Abram should have exercised his role as Sarai's husband and domestic priest by insisting that they refer the plan to God for His approval. It was his job to make sure that anything they might do to hurry along God's promise was not an act of unbelief. He could have gone to God and said, "You told me my own son would be my heir. Did you mean a son from my own wife, Sarai?"

   b. Instead of asking God to clarify the situation, Abram yielded to Sarai's urgency.

c. Knowing from our previous lesson that Abram had consciously put his faith in God for the promise of a son, we might be surprised that he did not stand up to Sarai. Yet this episode reveals just how human these people were. Perhaps Abram was intimidated by Sarai and wanted to avoid confrontation with her. Perhaps her doubts stirred up the embers of his own. Perhaps the reasonableness of her plan appealed to him. Perhaps he feared his life would be miserable unless he yielded to her. Perhaps, too, the enticement of sexual union with Hagar was hard to resist.

We cannot help but remember Eden in this episode. As Adam listened to Eve and ate the forbidden fruit, so Abram "hearkened to the voice of his wife" and departed from God's plan for them. What Sarai needed from Abram was the same thing Eve needed from Adam—a man who puts God first, no matter what the cost, whether it's facing a cunning serpent or an emotional, insistent wife.

3. Sarai's plan led almost immediately to disaster. Hagar looked down on Sarai, and Sarai blew up at Abram. She blamed him for the whole mess. Surely here was a husband who couldn't win—his wife insisted that he carry out her will, and when he did, she blamed him for the problems it created. Still, Abram had another chance to assert his role as head of the home. He could have taken the sorry problem to God; instead, he removed himself from it. By allowing Sarai to take care of things, he simply deepened the chaos within the household. In some ways, this is a living example of the effects of original sin on husbands and wives. When men fail in their leadership, some women are ready to usurp authority, with problematic results. No one is happy.

The Birth of Ishmael (Gen. 16:7–16)

4. a. Responses will vary. God always deals kindly with slaves. As we know from an earlier lesson, His own people would become slaves in Egypt so that they would comprehend how utterly dependent on Him they were. Indeed, the Incarnation was God's response of kindness to the captivity of sin that binds all descendants of Adam and Eve. In this episode, Hagar was especially helpless. She was used by Sarai to obtain a son, and then she was treated harshly when she offended her mistress. She ran away out of fear. God had pity on her in her desperation.

b. Hagar seemed humbly appreciative of this visit from God, marveling over the fact that she lived to talk about it. God met her in a situation not created by Him. Her pregnancy was not part of His plan for Abram. There would be long-lasting consequences of this action. Yet Hagar personally met God. He stooped down to relieve the affliction caused by Abram and Sarai. God never turns a blind eye to human suffering, even (perhaps especially) when it comes from human blundering.

Abram Becomes Abraham (Gen. 17:1–8)

5. *Challenge question*: Responses will vary. Each time in Genesis that God entered into a covenant with men, there was an explicit understanding that they were to live in a way that honors Him. With Adam and Eve, God's commands were more positive than negative—be fruitful, have dominion, and don't eat the forbidden fruit. With Noah, the commands were similar—be fruitful, have dominion, and respect life. When God formalized His earlier promise to make Abram's "name great" (Gen. 12:2) into a covenant, He told Abram to live his life blamelessly before Him. This perpetuates a pattern in God's covenants with men: God does a mighty thing, with mighty promises, and then requires a life appropriate to the great gift He has given man. In Eden, God blessed man and woman with life in a beautiful garden, with each other, with provision for their every need. They could preserve this blessing by obedience. With Noah, God preserved him and his family from utter destruction. He blessed them with all they needed; they could preserve this blessing by their obedience. With Abram, God opened heaven to heap up promises of blessings for him, his descendants, and all the earth. For his part, Abram would preserve the blessing by living his life before God in right-eousness, as God directed him here. To be "blameless" is to be "perfect." God wanted Abram's complete trust in Him, which is always a covenant requirement.

6. Abram fell down to the ground, in an act of complete reverence for God.

7. Responses will vary. In this appearance to Abram, God was about to do something in and through him that would create a new nation. Abram had lived for twenty-five years with God. He had occasionally stumbled, but he never turned back from God's call to trust Him. God was pleased with Abram's faith; He changed his name to reflect the fact that He was going to make of this faithful man "a multitude of nations." Perhaps it was necessary for Abram's faith to be tested before he would be ready to receive a new name like this. By living in Canaan for twenty-five years, he had left behind for good the life he once knew. Now, even his name would reflect the new life God gave him.

The Covenant of Circumcision (Gen. 17:9–21)

8. a. *Challenge question*: In asking Abraham to be circumcised, God asked him to temporarily disable his reproductive organ, even though Abraham was dependent on the birth of a son for all the promises of God to be fulfilled. Because of his advancing age, reason would suggest that Abraham should avoid doing anything that might put his ability to father a child in jeopardy. Abraham would have to believe that God would produce a son from him, no matter what his physical condition would be. In this, Abraham would have to believe in God's promises in the same way that the Blessed Virgin Mary did: "For with God nothing will be impossible" (Lk. 1:37).

b. Responses will vary. God's promises to Abraham all boiled down to one thing: the birth of a "miracle" child to an old man and his barren wife. Abraham was, as Saint Paul once described him, a man "as good as dead because he was about a hundred years old" (Rom. 4:19). Yet out of that "death," descendants more numer-ous than the stars were born. For Abraham to submit to circumcision, so close to the time when God promised that his son would be born, sealed this great reality forever into his mind and into the collective memory of Israel.

This was actually a very appropriate sign of how God works His will in the world. In circumcision, Abraham experienced pain, blood, suffering, and a period of impotence before God's great promises were fulfilled and a new nation was born. On the Cross, the Messiah of Israel experienced pain, blood, suffering and seeming impotence against His enemies, but the outcome was salvation for all mankind. Out of His suffering a new nation, the Church, was born. The sign of the New Covenant is Baptism, which is a fulfillment of circumcision. Although it involves water, which seems a far cry from pain, blood, suffering, and death, the Scripture tells us that in Baptism, we share in Christ's death. "Do you not know that all of us who have been baptized into Christ Jesus were baptized into his death?" (Rom. 6:3). Our share in Christ's death makes possible the promise of a share in His eternal life.

9. Responses will vary. It is hard to tell whether this is the laughter of amusement or of incredulity. Perhaps it was a mixture of both. The idea of Abraham and Sarah having a child in their advancing years was so outrageously wonderful to Abraham that it made him laugh. This kind of joy was something the apostles experienced when Jesus appeared in their midst after the Resurrection and they "disbelieved for joy" (see Lk. 24:36–41). To Abraham, it must have seemed like something too good to be true.

   Notice that Abraham made his comments to himself, not God. Perhaps he was trying to talk himself into believing what God had just promised. Then he asked God to make Ishmael his heir (see next question), which possibly suggests a certain ambivalence about it all.

   The picture of Abraham on the floor, laughing at the thought of fathering a child with Sarah, is not easy to evaluate. Was it an expression of delightful intimacy between God and Abraham? Was it an expression of irreverence? Interestingly, God told Abraham that the son to be born would be called "Isaac," which means "he laughed." Abraham would have a perpetual reminder of this episode of laughter. God, who works through reversal, would have the last "laugh."

10. Responses will vary. Ishmael, Abraham's only son, was thirteen years old. Surely Abraham loved him very much. Deep bonds of affection had developed between them. It isn't too surprising that Abraham longed for this beloved child to be the one through whom God worked. This was not necessarily a lack of faith on Abraham's part. It may simply have been the expression of his attachment to his son, which is a natural human instinct. One of the consequences of Abraham's lapse with Hagar was that he would have to suffer the agony of detaching himself from Ishmael. This would be very difficult. It represents the kind of temporal suffering we introduce into our lives by departing from God's plan.

Abraham Obeys God (Gen. 17:22–27)

11. Imagine Abraham's possible line of thought—God had told him that Sarah would give birth in another year, but circumcision would prevent any natural means of conception for a time. His human reason might have told him this was no way to have a son, but his prompt obedience was a strong sign of his desire to please God, no matter what his misgivings might have been.

Lesson 5

To make the most of this study, respond to all the questions yourself before reading these responses.

Three Visitors (Gen. 18:1–15)

1. a. Abraham was the picture of hospitality to the three visitors. He showed them respect and energetically made himself and his goods entirely available to them, holding nothing back.

b. *Challenge question*: According to Jesus, welcoming strangers as Abraham did is one of the behaviors characteristic of those who will enter the kingdom of God. Jesus connected our treatment of others to our treatment of Him. To show respect for the human creatures God has made is to show respect to Him. Hospitality to strangers is a profoundly human expression of our love of God. As the passage in Hebrews reminds us, hospitality to strangers can open the door to unthinkable blessing.

2. a. Sarah seemed to be amused by the idea that after years of barrenness (and possibly a cessation in the act of conjugal love), she and Abraham could enjoy "pleasure" again.

b. Responses will vary. Sarah's laugh may have been a mixture of delight and incredulity, much like Abraham's laugh. The thought of having pleasure with Abraham and having a son in her old age perhaps seemed too good to be true. Sarah may have been trying to cover up her doubt when she denied she had laughed. The angel assured her that nothing is too hard for the Lord.

Abraham Prays for Deliverance (Gen. 18:16–33)

2. a. God wanted Abraham to know Him very well, to be deeply acquainted with how He works in the world. Abraham would have the role of teacher, example, and mediator of God's blessing to his descendants and all the earth. He had this role as a result of his calling or "election" ("I have chosen him," v. 19). He was to teach his descendants how "to keep the way of the Lord by doing righteousness and justice" (v. 19). This would be important because if Abraham's descendants lived righteously with God, by following Abraham's example, then God could fulfill all His covenant promises to them.

All of this puts us on alert about what comes next. We understand that whatever was about to transpire between God and Abraham was meant to do several things: (1) It would teach Abraham something about justice and righteousness; (2) It would make him an example of how the elect (or "chosen") are to live their lives with God.

b. God intended to test the people of Sodom by visiting them (that is what "I will go down to see" means, v. 21). He made reference to an "outcry" that had come to Him (v. 21). Who had made this outcry? Was it Lot? Was it some of the inhabitants of the city? We don't know. The outcry, however God received it, caused Him to visit the city to verify the gravity of the charge against them.

4. a. Responses will vary. Abraham stood still, then drew near to the Lord. Perhaps he was mulling over what the Lord had said and what the implications were. Was he thinking about Lot and his family? Was he wondering if and what he should say to the Lord? Surely his mind churned.

b. Abraham did not want to think that God would destroy the righteous with the wicked.

c. *Challenge question*: Abraham was confident in God's justice. He did not believe that God would allow the righteous to suffer the same fate as the wicked. Abraham comprehended in a flash that if the Creator of the world is not just, men are in very serious trouble ("Far be it from thee to do such a thing. . . . Far be that from thee!" v. 25). Why? Because if the Creator is not just, then there is no difference between right and wrong. If God does not reward righteousness and punish wickedness, men can and will do whatever they want. The alternative to justice is chaos.

This request from Abraham revealed him to be a man who believed that God is just and that He can be expected to deal justly with men. It was his confidence in God's true character that made him bold in his appeal.

5. Responses will vary. Abraham was a combination of boldness and humility, tenacity and deference, fearlessness and reverence. His urgency, confidence, and level of intimacy with the Lord did not lead to presumption, grasping, or impropriety. He was fully engaged in this great moment with God, but he did not think of himself as the center of it. This made him an effective and persuasive mediator.

Angels Visit Lot (Gen. 19:1–14)

6. Responses will vary. Lot offered the visitors the same kind of hospitality that Abraham did. Although he may not have known who they were, perhaps there was something in their appearance that made Lot recognize that the streets of Sodom would not be a good place for them to spend the night. He wanted them to be on their way quickly out of the city ("you may rise up early and go on your way," v. 2). Lot was not only aware of the wickedness of Sodom, he also wanted to protect the visitors from experiencing it, which was noble.

7. Responses will vary. Lot knew right from wrong, but he seemed cowardly in resisting the wicked men at his door. He seemed weak and fearful in the face of their lust.

8. The men at the door resented Lot's judgment on their behavior. Their anger was directed towards him not for denying them what they wanted but for daring to "play the judge" among them, even though he was an outsider. This reveals the pride that lay at the heart of their wickedness. Pride is a greater sin than lust. Lust is a disordered appetite; pride strikes at God's authority over us. "[H]atred of God comes from pride. It is contrary to love of God, whose goodness it denies, and whom it presumes to curse as the one who forbids sin and inflicts punishments" (*Catechism*, no. 2094).

Sodom and Gomorrah Destroyed (Gen. 19:15–38)

9. a. Responses will vary. In this account of Lot's deliverance from Sodom, it is hard to avoid feeling a certain distaste for him. He did not fall into the category of "wicked," because he did try to protect the visitors from any contact with the Sodomites. He was willing to rebuke them for their behavior. He listened to the angels' warning to flee, but in the last moment, he hesitated. He was dragged out of the city, by God's mercy (see 19:16).

Once out of the city, Lot caved in to fear. He would not go to the mountains, as the angels instructed him, but he requested instead to be allowed to go to Zoar, a small city in the valley. He feared that in the mountains, he might be overtaken by some "disaster." But even in Zoar, he still lived in fear, so he fled to a cave with his two daughters. After the incestuous incidents with his daughters, we don't hear about Lot again in Genesis. He leaves us shaking our heads.

Lot spent many years living in a place of renowned wickedness. Presumably he married a woman from Sodom. Did he have much contact with Abraham? Probably not, although his uncle valiantly rescued him when he got into trouble. When we meet him again in this chapter, he shows himself to be a man whose righteousness was weak and tenuous. The New Testament describes him as one who was righteously indignant over the wickedness of Sodom (see 2 Pet. 2:4–10), and we have seen evidence of that. However, his virtue was somewhat short of heroic! Lot appears to have been the kind of man Saint Paul described once in a letter to the Corinthians: "Now if any one builds on the foundation with gold, silver, precious stones, wood, hay, straw—each man's work will become manifest; for the Day will disclose it, because it will be revealed with fire, and the fire will test what sort of work each one has done. If the work which any man has built on the foundation survives, he will receive a reward. If any man's work is burned up, he will suffer loss, though he himself will be saved, but only as through fire" (1 Cor. 3:12–15). Lot was saved, by God's grace, but barely.

b. The Lord "remembered Abraham" (v. 29)—how Abraham had urgently pleaded with Him to spare the righteous—so He sent Lot out of the city. Even though Lot hesitated, God acted. The Lord's regard for Abraham saved Lot's life.

10. *Challenge question*: Responses will vary. Abraham serves as an example of how a man lives as a covenant-keeper with God:

- Covenant-keepers should occasionally expect to be visited by God in "disguise." Energetic hospitality is the proper response to these visits. Sometimes He may come to us "hidden" in a family member, a co-worker, or a stranger in need. Abraham's respect for and self-donation on behalf of his three visitors show us the way to "entertain angels unaware."
- Covenant-keepers can expect that sometimes God will ordain circumstances in our lives that are meant to be occasions for Him to reveal His

nature to us. These circumstances will cause us to examine what we believe about God—who He is and how He acts in the world. Covenant-keepers will defend God's character against accusations or doubts (even when they come from within), just as Abraham did.

- Covenant-keepers should see themselves as God's coworkers, just as God described Abraham as one through whom the whole earth would be blessed. We should be prepared to pray as intercessors for those who are in need of God's mercy. God's deliverance of Lot from Sodom because He "remembered Abraham" (v. 29) shows us the power of prayers from God's covenant people.

- Covenant-keepers should be as bold and as humble as Abraham was before God.

Lesson 6

To make the most of this study, respond to all the questions yourself before reading these responses.

Abraham and Abimelech (Gen. 20:1–18)

1. Responses will vary. Anyone who has done the same wrong thing twice can imagine how Abraham got here again. Fear gripped him, and he resorted to the most expedient way of preserving his life. What might have been going through his mind? "Surely God knows why I have to do this. Surely He will forgive me for it. He doesn't want me dead! I'm sure He'll understand." Any of us who have done what we know is wrong to do, even in a small thing, will be familiar with this line of thinking. It is the beginning of presumption, which, when it starts small this way, is always at its most lethal. Those in positions of authority, those with superior knowledge and experiences, and those who have been abundantly blessed by God are perhaps those most vulnerable to it. The problem with even small episodes of presumption lies in the devious and subtle nature of sin. We always believe we have control over it and can break out of it when we want to. "Just this one time" reflects that kind of gullibility. But Saint Paul accurately described the power of sin as that of a slave master. When we give into it, we lose our freedom from it. "What then? Are we to sin because we are. . . under grace? By no means! Do you not know that if you yield yourselves to any one as obedient slaves, you are slaves of the one whom you obey, either of sin, which leads to death, or of obedience, which leads to righteousness?" (Rom. 6:15–16). The power of sin to enslave is formidable.

This evidence of possible presumption in Abraham is something worth watching.

2. a. Responses will vary. There was some urgency for the release of Sarah. God appeared to the one who was able to make that happen.

b. Responses will vary. Although Abimelech suggested that his hands were entirely clean, God reminded him that it took a special intervention to prevent "a near occasion of sin" from turning into actual sin. And how did Abimelech position himself to this near occasion of sin? It was by his abduction of Sarah from Abraham. Why take even a "sister" from a "brother," if not for selfish purposes? Abimelech had no claim on Sarah. That was his offense.

3. God promised Abraham that within a year a son would be born to Sarah. Any sexual contact that Sarah had with anyone other than Abraham might cast doubt on the legitimacy of that birth. God did not let that happen. He preserved His plan to give Sarah a son from Abraham.

4. Abimelech had legitimate anger against Abraham for his deception, since it was the cause of his illness and the threat of death. It wouldn't have been unreasonable for him to think, "Can't God find better quality people to do His work?" Imagine having to ask for prayers that will save your life from the very one who got you into trouble in the first place. Yet God told Abimelech that Abraham was a "prophet" (the simplest meaning of the word "prophet" is "one who speaks for God") and that healing would be mediated through the prayers of this prophet, flawed as he was.

The Birth of Isaac (Gen. 21:1–7)

5. Responses will vary. Sometimes the deepest kind of joy in our lives comes over the things that at one time seemed the most impossible. When Sarah first laughed at the idea of having a child after so many years of being barren and Abraham being so old, there must have been a good bit of incredulity in it, or she would not have tried to deny it. When her son was born, he became the living proof that God keeps His promises, no matter how impossible they seem. Sarah's attitude towards God must have grown from reverent respect (she feared she would be in trouble if she acknowledged her laugh) to deep love for and confidence in Him as she held her son in her arms. The birth of this child, for Sarah, was not just a demonstration of God's power and trustworthiness. It was a profoundly personal expression of His love for her ("God has made laughter for me"). She seems to have been liberated by this encounter with Him, for now she envisions others sharing her laughter of delight, with no need to deny it. The laughter will be a response to an unthinkable reversal—that which had seemed too good to be true actually happened.

Sarah's prophetic word about the effect that the news of the birth of her son will have on "every one who hears" is a foreshadowing of Mary's prophetic word about the effect of the news of the birth of her Son: "All generations will call me blessed" (Lk. 1:48). The mother of Israel foreshadows the Mother of the Church.

A Problem over Ishmael (Gen. 21:8–21)

6. Sarah probably could see the handwriting on the wall. Ishmael, as Abraham's first born son, would try to pull rank on Isaac. If this were allowed to fester, it would undoubtedly present problems for the fulfillment of God's promise to Abraham to make a great nation of him through Sarah's son. What kind of rights as the first-born would Ishmael have? Would he receive the patriarchal blessing instead of Isaac? Would Ishmael continue to harass Isaac, especially if Isaac's unique role as the child of promise in the family became clear with time? It is not hard to see why Sarah urged Abraham to take action.

7. Abraham loved Ishmael. His affections were deeply attached to the boy, which would be normal. It would cause him agony to lose him and his mother. That pain, of course, would be the consequence of a mistake made long ago. To do God's will by making Isaac his sole heir would require a kind of death for Abraham. It would mean facing up to the weakness that had developed in his heart for Ishmael. It was a moment of decision.

8. *Challenge question*: It appears that Abraham took Sarah's idea to God; verse 12 seems to be God's end of a conversation Abraham was having with Him. This time, God had an opportunity to respond to Sarah's suggestion. Surprisingly, perhaps, to Abraham, this time Sarah was right.

9. a. This severe action suggests that Abraham's weakness concerning Ishmael was significant. He had shown himself in the past to be very attached to him; perhaps this attachment would threaten Abraham's resolve to follow through with the terms of the covenant he had made with God to make Isaac his heir. Maybe there was some deep ambivalence in his heart about Ishmael. The harsh remedy was the most effective way of getting to the root of this kind of weakness. It was severe but necessary.

God promised to be merciful to Hagar and Ishmael, which must have eased Abraham's mind somewhat. One has to wonder, though, why Abraham gave only bread and a skin of water to them when they set out from the camp.

b. Responses will vary. Perhaps Abraham secretly hoped they would have to quickly return when the food ran out. If so, there was half-heartedness in his obedience to God's command.

c. Responses will vary. God loved Abraham and everyone loved by Abraham (remember Lot). He showed great mercy to Hagar and Ishmael because of their relationship to Abraham. In addition, God is ever the friend of slaves, the helpless, and the abandoned (see Jas. 1:27).

A Covenant with Abimelech (Gen. 21:22–34)

10. Although Abraham must have been an impressive figure, Abimelech wanted to establish honesty and loyalty between them. This may be a veiled reference to Abraham's earlier deception concerning Sarah. In any case, Abraham agreed to deal honorably with Abimelech and his family. The men made a formal agreement, a covenant. This is the first time in Scripture we see a covenant being made among men; before this they have been initiated by God. This is not to suggest that men did not make covenants until this time; rather, it suggests that what men do among themselves to secure peace and well-being is actually a reflection of God's own nature, who continually extends to man the opportunity to live as a member of His family, in covenant with Him.

11. *Challenge question*: Responses will vary. We know from previous chapters that Abraham was a man of faith, a friend of God. We also know that he wasn't perfect. He has both inspired and disappointed us. He lived with God for more than twenty-five years by the time we reach these chapters. He had not turned back from following Him or trusting in His promises, but he stumbled and stalled out a few times.

In Genesis 20–21, we have a chance to ponder some of the weaknesses we see in Abraham. He lied about his relationship with Sarah and got both of them in trouble—again. Rather than learning from his earlier misstep, Abraham repeated it. Did a subtle presumption on his part make that possible? In addition, Abraham's heart was so attached to Ishmael that he found it very hard to part with the boy. His weakness for him made it necessary for God to send Ishmael and Hagar away. Even when he obeyed, it was a half-hearted obedience. Seeing these weaknesses in a man who had lived with God such a long time makes us wonder: is this the man through whom God promised to bless the whole world?

Lesson 7

To make the most of this study, respond to all the questions yourself before reading these responses.

A Shocking Command (Gen. 22:1–8)

1. Responses will vary. We see in Genesis 22:1 that "after these things," God tested Abraham. "These things" may refer to the events recorded in the previous two chapters. That would include the episode of Abraham's dishonesty about Sarah and his weakness for Ishmael, wanting to hold onto him instead of letting him go. Perhaps "these things" were serious enough in his life to require God to examine Abraham's faith. Recall that in Genesis 17:1, God had said to Abraham, "Walk before me, and be blameless." Although he had not repudiated God or forsaken the covenant, was he still willing to walk before God that way? A test would make this clear.

2. Responses will vary. We have no record of how Abraham reacted to this command from God. Did he walk out and take a look at the stars again, remembering how the sight of them had once before helped him to put his trust in God? Think of the objections that may have raced through his head. "You can't possibly mean this! The boy is everything to me. Have I lived with You so long, only to be required to do something worse than giving up my own life? Who are You, anyway? I thought You were better than the gods to whom people sacrifice their children. Has all this 'covenant' talk about descendants and a great nation and blessing the whole world through me just been a hoax? Why are You doing this to me? Is there any way I can change Your mind?"

Abraham could have had an outburst of emotion like this, directed towards God with the intention of negotiating a way out. He could also have decided that by no means was he going to lose another son to the whim of this God. He could have awakened the household, packed up, and fled with the boy in the darkness of night. "Forget all Your promises; they don't mean anything to me if I have to lose my son. You've asked too much this time."

Another possibility is that Abraham, shocked by God's command, could have begun a time of serious recollection of his friendship with God up to this point. "I am stunned by what You are asking of me. But during all the years I have lived with You, I have had many experiences of Your love, goodness, protection, faithfulness, mercy, and justice. You have asked me to do difficult things before, but no matter how hard they were, You always used them as occasions to bless me and my family. Leaving Haran and my father's house was no picnic, but You were with me every step of the way. Getting circumcised was painful and risky, but Sarah conceived and gave birth at the precise time You promised. But this—offering up my son. I cannot see how anything good can come of it. I'm afraid."

What a long night that must have been.

3. Responses will vary. Abraham must have gotten to the point of believing that God knew what He was doing, no matter how bad things might look. He trusted God more than he trusted himself, which is the essence of humility (and the opposite of presumption). He must have decided that it was better to let go of Isaac than to disobey God, in spite of the dread he must have felt at what lay ahead. As much as he loved this boy, he must have decided to love God more. He held nothing back.

4. *Challenge question*: The Hebrews reference to Abraham's word to his men about going to worship and returning suggests that Abraham believed that somehow, someway, his son would live on, even if that meant something as outrageous as a resurrection from the dead. How could he have come to a conclusion like that? Perhaps he reasoned along these lines: "God is asking me to sacrifice my son. I do not understand why, but I know I cannot refuse Him. Whatever God's reasons are, they must be good. Whatever happens, I know I can trust Him to keep His Word to me to give me descendants through this boy. Even if God has to raise Isaac from the dead, I know I will not return from Mount Moriah alone."

5. Abraham's focus was entirely on God. He did not appear to be thinking sentimental thoughts about Isaac. He did not break down in sobs when Isaac question him, or cry out, "Don't ask! Just don't ask!" He resolutely anchored everything that was about to happen in the will and action of God. It appears that all the jumble of emotions and questions that any normal person would experience in a situation like this had all been reduced to a single conviction: God is in charge here.

Salvation through Substitution (Gen. 22:9–14)

6. Responses will vary. It seems that the slow, detailed account of this episode is meant to give anyone who hears or reads it plenty of time to comprehend what a difficult, radical sacrifice Abraham was offering to God. The pathos of the scene has lots of time to build. Reading it with the benefit of New Testament revelation, we are able to experience its double significance. Not only can we enter into Abraham's mind and heart (as well as Isaac's), we are also able to look into the heart of God Himself, Who gave up His only beloved Son to a brutal, slow death on our behalf (see Rom. 8:32).

7. *Challenge question*: Responses will vary. When we compare the severity of this test to what seem like minor imperfections in Abraham, we ought to be curious about it. It should make us wonder, "What does God expect from His chosen

ones—perfection?" Actually, that is exactly what He desires for them. Why? Because a life of perfection is a life of perfect happiness. God's command to Abraham in Genesis 17:1 to "walk before me, and be blameless" was not simply a requirement. It was a description of how the members of God's family ought to live so that they can know the joy and fulfillment of living in perfect harmony with the end for which they were created, which is to be pleasing in God's sight and blessed by Him.

The test that God gave Abraham was so severe that it presumed an advanced level of knowledge and experience of Him. Compare it to the relatively simple test that God first put Abraham through, back in Genesis 12:1–4. There it was simply, "Pack up and go." Here, at least thirty years later, the test was staggeringly difficult. It built on everything that had gone before in Abraham's life. For Abraham to endure the test, he would have to act on all that he knew about God, and he would have to be willing to mortify even the smallest weaknesses and imperfections yet remaining in his character.

This is what we call "purification." It was the final step in Abraham's life that established him as the father of faith, both for Jews and Gentiles (Rom. 4:11–12). His obedience burned away the dross of even relatively minor imperfections. Interestingly, the test of Abraham gives us a dramatic demonstration of why God tests men, as He tested the first man, Adam. Men must freely choose to lay down their own wills in order to serve God. When they do this, they are conformed to the likeness of God. They participate in self-donation, which is the essence of the life of the Blessed Trinity. Abraham not only obeyed God, but he became a living example of the character of God; he was a human being who reflected both the image and likeness of God. As the *Catechism* says, "As a final stage in the purification of his faith, Abraham, 'who had received the promises' [Heb. 11:17], is asked to sacrifice the son God had given him. . . . And so the father of believers is conformed to the likeness of the Father who will not spare his own Son, but will deliver him up for us all [Rom 8:32]" (no. 2572). When we see Abraham, we see the Father. God tests men to divinize them.

8. *Challenge question*: The reference in John may be a wonderfully mysterious allusion to that dramatic moment on Mount Moriah, when the angel stayed Abraham's hand from sacrificing his son. When he lifted his eyes to see the ram in the thicket, was he able to "see" the day when God would provide the perfect sacrifice, His own dear Son, crowned with thorns, on the altar of Calvary? Was it a mystical vision of future glory that he "saw"? The words of Jesus point in that direction.

God Swears an Oath (Gen. 22:15–24)

9. Abraham's obedience prompted God to swear an oath, with which He vowed to open the floodgates of heaven for blessings. The oath made God's covenant irrevocable. He was sworn to bless "all the nations" through Abraham, so pleased was He with this act of obedience on Moriah. In swearing that oath, He also took on Himself the covenant curse, if ever it was broken. As Scott Hahn writes,

> By swearing an oath, [God] voluntarily put himself under a curse. God thus declared his intention to do whatever it takes to bless us, even if that

means bearing the curse of death for our sin. This may help us to understand the Father's purpose in commanding Abraham to offer Isaac. In effect, he called Abraham to show the world what was needed to take away our sin, that is, a faithful father who offers his only beloved son as a holocaust atop Moriah. This also clarifies why God prevented Abraham from carrying out the sacrifice, since the world's salvation required nothing less than the offering of the God-man, Jesus Christ, the "seed of Abraham" (see Gal. 3:14–19).[1]

10. a. *Challenge question*: Hebrews 11 says that "strangers and exiles on the earth" (v. 13) are looking for a heavenly homeland. They have their hearts set on the city "which has foundations, whose builder and maker is God" (v. 10). Nothing on earth will satisfy.

b. Responses will vary. Perhaps Abraham's experience with God on Mount Moriah was so dramatic that everything else seemed thin and temporary next to it. Perhaps he could "see" something of the glory of life with God, and it left him longing for more. Undergoing such intense purification, Abraham may have experienced what mystical theology calls the "transforming union" with God. Nothing is ever the same afterwards. There is no home but heaven.

Lesson 8
To make the most of this study, respond to all the questions yourself before reading these responses.

Jacob and Esau (Gen. 25:19–34)
1. a. Rebekah went to the Lord to find the source and meaning of the discord in her womb.

b. God told her that the twins she was carrying would father two nations. They would be unequal in strength, and the older would serve the younger. This revelation accurately predicted the future relationship between Israel and Edom, the nations that would spring from her sons.

c. Jacob, "he takes by the heel" or "he supplants," grabbed his twin by the heel as though trying to pull his way out first. Jacob would find it difficult to leave things to God, striving instead to work circumstances to his own advantage and pull ahead by wiliness and his own effort.

2. a. Esau was interested only in satisfying his own immediate needs. The value of his birthright would have to wait years to be realized. Thus, the pressing appetite of his body blotted out the deferred joy of his birthright. In the heat of the moment, he sold his future for a meal.

---

[1] Scott Hahn, *A Father Who Keeps His Promises* (Ann Arbor, MI: Servant Publications, 1998), 109.

b. Esau's first priority was himself, and the needs and pleasures of the moment, whereas Jacob would do whatever it took to get the future, lasting benefit that the birthright would provide.

3. *Challenge question*: God chose Jacob because He wanted to choose Jacob—not because of anything Jacob had done, good or bad. This is clear because Jacob was chosen over his twin even before they were born. Jacob would be the son born second, without any natural rights. God chose the one who had no real claim on it to inherit the birthright from Isaac.

Jacob was chosen, as Saint Paul says, "in order that God's purpose in election might stand: not by works but by him who calls." God was teaching His people about grace: those who don't really deserve it are its recipients. No one can do anything to earn God's favor—no one. Just as Jacob, the younger son, didn't deserve the birthright but got it, we don't deserve God's blessings, but He gives them to us. This is the principle of election, which says that God's choice depends on His sovereign will and mercy toward us. The *Catechism* tells us that God had "a single motive for choosing them from among all peoples. . . : his sheer gratuitous love [Jn. 18:37]" (no. 218).

Rebekah's Plot (Gen. 27:1–17)

4. a. Rebekah loved Jacob more than his brother. Why was that? We don't know for sure, but Genesis 25:27–28 tells us that "When the boys grew up, Esau was a skillful hunter, a man of the field, while Jacob was a quiet man, dwelling in tents. Isaac loved Esau, because he ate of his game; but Rebekah loved Jacob." Perhaps the bitterness caused by Esau's foreign wives had eaten away at her. When she heard Isaac's plan to bless Esau, she panicked. She knew that God had promised that "the elder shall serve the younger" (Gen. 25:23), so she took the situation into her own hands. She was determined that Jacob—and not Esau—would get his father's blessing. She was even willing to take the risk of being cursed to make sure he got it (Gen. 27:13).

b. Scripture does not justify Rebekah's scheme or Jacob's deception. They did not give God time to work out the plan He had promised. It happened, of course, but instead of letting God do it His way, both Rebekah and Jacob experienced bitter fruit from their meddling. Jacob had to flee his home, and Rebekah died without ever seeing her favorite son again. (That God does not need to use such means will become evident in Genesis 48, when a younger twin is blessed over the older—by a blind Jacob this time—without any trickery or double–dealing.)

Jacob Steals Isaac's Blessing (Gen. 27:18–40)

5. a. Esau wanted any scrap of blessing he could get for himself from Isaac. He was justifiably angry, of course, but his anger was not because of what had been done to his father. He was furious over losing the blessing for himself. He spent no time at all comforting his father, who "trembled violently" when he realized what had happened. Esau thought only of himself and what he had lost. Then his wrath turned towards Jacob.

b. Esau said that Jacob had taken away his birthright. The truth was that Esau had thought so little of it that he sold it to Jacob for a meal. There had been no deception in that deal at all. Esau had not been a victim of Jacob's trickery.

c. *Challenge question*: Unfortunately, they were not the tears of repentance. Instead of being shocked into realizing how both he and Jacob had been less than perfect sons, Esau cast all the blame on Jacob. He missed a wonderful opportunity for humility and repentance. The tears he shed were only for himself and his loss. That is why Hebrews 12:17 tells us that he was "rejected," in spite of his tears.

"Why Should I Be Bereft of You Both in One Day?" (Gen. 27:41–28:9)
6. a. Rebekah complained to Isaac that Esau's Hittite wives were ruining her life. She worried out loud about what would happen if Jacob also married a Hittite woman. This prompted Isaac to send Jacob off to search for a wife among Abraham's people. Rebekah manipulated Isaac into doing what she thought was necessary. Miraculously, in spite of all his mischief, Isaac sent Jacob away with God's blessing.

b. Esau heard Isaac say, "You shall not marry one of the Canaanite women." He observed how pleased Isaac and Rebekah were that Jacob was returning to the people of Abraham. It must have looked like a fresh start for all of them, something they all desperately needed. Perhaps Esau decided it was time for him to make a fresh start, too. He went to Ishmael, Abraham's other son, and took one of his daughters as a wife. Was it a small step in the right direction, or was it yet another attempt to gain a blessing from Isaac? Time will tell.

Jacob Flees (Gen. 28:10–22)
7. a. Responses will vary. God revealed Himself to Jacob as "the Lord, the God of your father Abraham and the God of Isaac." This said to Jacob far more than that God is great and powerful: it told him that He is a personal God, a God who seeks out men to bless them. God assured Jacob that He intended to keep all the promises He had made to Abraham to bless him and his descendants. He promised to be with him wherever he went and to bring him back safely to the land he now had to flee.

b. Jacob's dream convinced him that God would care for him on his journey and bring him back to Canaan. He understood that a God who is that personal deserves a personal response. So he vowed that because God would care for him so wonderfully well, when he returned to the land he was now leaving, he would give Him a tenth of all he possessed. It was a promise to worship God, to give to God instead of trying to get from Him. It was, in fact, the beginning of Jacob's conversion.

Lesson 9

To make the most of this study, respond to all the questions yourself before reading these responses.

Jacob Heads Home (Gen. 32:1–21)

1. a. Responses will vary. Jacob must have remembered Esau's vow to kill him once their father had died. He must have wondered if all the years had given Esau time to brood and plot over what he would do if he ever laid eyes on Jacob again. Would there be a burst of pent-up rage? Did Jacob dread being reminded of his deceit in stealing the blessing from his brother? Would he be tempted to resort to intrigue again when it came time for him to "rule" over Esau, as God had told Rebekah so long ago? Jacob had many good reasons to expect an unpleasant, difficult reception from Esau.

b. The angels of God, last seen at Bethel as Jacob was fleeing Esau, met Jacob as he left Gilead and camped alongside him (Mahanaim means "camps"). The presence of God's army must have been an enormous assurance as he prepared to face Esau again. It was a tangible reminder that God had promised to bring him safely back to Canaan, evidence that He had not forgotten.

c. What Jacob did with his fear shows how much he had changed in twenty years. He took immediate action to protect his family and herds by dividing them up, and then attempted to pacify his brother and perhaps hold him off a bit by sending ahead a series of herds as gifts to him. But most importantly, he prayed. He prayed to the God of his fathers, whom he recognized as the God who told him to take this trip and promised to be with him.

What Jacob prayed was important, but it was equally important *that* he prayed. The young Jacob longed for what God promised him, and he did anything and everything in his power to get it. The mature Jacob continued to want what God had for him and did what was prudent to move ahead, but his prayer shows that he knew he was in God's hands. We can learn from Jacob's example. "Prayer is a vital necessity," the *Catechism* tells us. It and "Christian life are inseparable" (nos. 2744–45).

d. Responses will vary. Jacob had twenty years to learn how to live with God as a covenant man. The dream at Bethel had been the beginning of his conversion to the God of his fathers. Once he opened his life to God personally, he learned lessons of humility, trust in God, and obedience to Him, through all his ups and downs in Haran. Jacob's relationship with God had deepened as a result of his trials. Every setback must have turned him towards God, with simple prayers like "Help!" or "What now?" or "Are You still there?" The only way Jacob could have become the man he was when he returned to Canaan was by years of almost imperceptible but steady growth in his faith. At Bethel, Jacob had opened the door of his life to God. In Haran, God went through that door and made Himself at home.

A New Name and a Blessing (Gen. 32:22–32)

2. a. Jacob may have thought the man was a spy for his brother. He may have feared that all his concerns about seeing his brother again had been well founded. Now that he was completely alone, here was this intruder to take out his brother's revenge on him. It was probably a very tense encounter.

b. When "the man" touched Jacob's thigh, putting it out of joint, Jacob knew this was no ordinary man. A man who wrestles all night but who can put a man's thigh out with just a "touch" is most extraordinary! Jacob understood in a flash that this "man" was the true presence of God Himself.

c. Responses will vary. When Jacob recognized the identity of the stranger, he must have wondered why on earth (or in heaven) God had met him in such a mysterious way. If Jacob were God's covenant man, why did He treat him like an opponent? If Jacob trusted God for deliverance in the very delicate situation with Esau, why would He cripple him right before the biggest day of his life? Jacob had lots of reasons to be very confused by this encounter with God—confused and full of questions.

d. Even though Jacob must have been deeply curious about what was happening to him, he knew enough to ask for a blessing. He understood that this moment was very important—he was locked in combat with Yahweh, and he insisted on having a blessing from Him. Somehow, he was able to look beyond the immediate details and whatever questions he had about them. He knew that, in spite of appearances, there was something good available for him here.

3. a. Responses will vary. The last time Jacob had sought a covenant "blessing," he had deceived his father about his identity: "Who are you, my son?" Isaac asked. "Jacob said to his father, 'I am Esau your first-born'" (Gen. 27:18–19). This time, in order to get the blessing he sought, he had to say his name—his own name—out loud to get it. No more lying and trickery. This was a blessing sought with integrity.

b. Responses will vary. Jacob got a name change because he was a new man as a result of his wrestling match with God. Although he had been crippled, he refused to let go of his divine opponent until he received a blessing. Jacob had good reason to be disappointed by the way God had answered his prayer, but he blindly hung on to Him for "the good" he had asked in that prayer. Jacob never gave up in his holy struggle, and this pleased God immensely. His tenacity, courage, and faith were rewarded by a new name, which would forever mark Jacob's new relationship with God. He was now, truly, a man of the covenant.

c. Responses will vary. The "man" wanted to know why Jacob would need to ask His name. Jacob already knew who this was, because of the touch on his thigh. Beyond that, the "man" did not want to go. As the *Catechism* tells us, God is slow to give Himself a name in Scripture. God's name is shrouded in mystery; it is too great for us to comprehend. He cannot be encompassed within the meaning of a name. This reluctance to name Himself reminded Jacob that although he and God had wrestled, they were not equals.

4. Jacob knew that something momentous had happened in his relationship with God. He had drawn close to God—dangerously close—and yet his life had been preserved. He wasn't completely unscathed, since the limp in his leg would remind him of God's power over him. Yet God had made it possible for Jacob to enter into dramatic intimacy with Himself and not die. He received what mattered most to him—the blessing of God. The name Jacob gave the place, Peniel, expressed his awe and gratitude for so great a gift.

Jacob Confronts Esau (Gen. 33:1–11)

5. Jacob began "bowing himself to the ground" long before Esau ever got near to him. Seven times he went down, before he reached his brother. Esau could have seen, even from a distance, that Jacob was returning in humility. He behaved as if he were Esau's servant, not the brother who possessed his father's birthright and blessing. Jacob made sure that Esau recognized that his return was full of repentance, not triumph. He had not come home to lord it over his brother; he had come seeking reconciliation.

6. a. Responses will vary. Had time cured the wound inflicted on Esau by his brother's deception? Had Esau watched his mother die in deep grief over never again seeing the son who had to flee his brother's wrath? Had he begun to regret the anger that had driven Jacob away? When he had taken a daughter of Ishmael for his wife (Gen. 28:8–9) to please his parents, was that a first step towards putting his family first? What effect did the scene of Jacob bowing down over and over have on him? No wonder he couldn't hold back the tears whey they finally embraced!

b. Jacob wanted to give gifts to Esau instead of taking something from him, as he had done before. Esau, for his part, did not want to take anything from his brother, a far cry from the last time he saw him, when he begged his father to give him some of the blessing given to Jacob. The brothers' hearts were generous, not self-seeking and miserly. Their love liberated them from their possessions and their pride.

7. *Challenge question*: Responses will vary. Jacob's statement to Esau was an incredibly beautiful way for him to express the joy of his return to the land of Canaan, the land of the covenant and the land where all God's promises to his ancestors and to him would be kept. The family of Isaac, Abraham's beloved son, had been reunited. Old hurts had been buried; both men were wiser for all their missteps. Jacob was ready to begin the life God had planned for him, as the younger who would rule the elder. Jacob was finally home, and that's why seeing Esau's face was like seeing the face of God.

Return to Bethel (Gen. 35:1–15)

8. a. Jacob must have realized that there was chaos in his household. Surely he regretted his decision not to journey on to Bethel but to stop in Shechem. His sons had hideously misunderstood the meaning of circumcision, because they had used it as a trick to overpower the Shechemites. Circumcision had been the sign of God's covenant with Abraham and his descendants. It was not to be cheapened and abused in the way his sons had done. Jacob knew that he had to restore order in his family. He needed to provide them with leadership, rather than passively capitulate to his sons' passions. He knew it was time to renew his commitment to live the birthright he had gotten from Esau. He wanted to cleanse his family of any influence of idolatry, present among them because of the idols Rachel had stolen from her father. Those were buried, and clean clothes were put on, to symbolize their repentance and return to the covenant. All of these instructions had one purpose: to make a fresh start with God.

b. *Challenge question*: God sent Jacob back to Bethel to renew the covenant with him. He let Jacob know that in spite of weakness, compromise, and failure in his family life, this was indeed the family God would use to fulfill all His promises to Abraham. God had told Jacob in a dream that one day he would return to the land he then had to flee, and that return would mark the beginning of his life as Isaac's heir.

Jacob's altar at Bethel, where he worshipped the God who "had spoken with him" (Gen. 35:15), began his fulfillment of the vow he had made to God there so many years before: "the LORD shall be my God" (28:21).

Lesson 10

To make the most of this study, respond to all the questions yourself before reading these responses.

Joseph and His Dreams (Gen. 37:1–11)

1. a. Responses will vary. Joseph's brothers hated him because their father loved him above all his other children. The brothers deeply resented him for this special favor of the father on the son, made palpable in the "long robe with sleeves" that Jacob made for Joseph. The elegance of the robe set Joseph apart, almost as a prince among his brothers. This special status in one so young made them so angry they "could not speak peaceably to him" (v. 4).

b. Responses will vary. Joseph "brought an ill report" of his brothers to his father. We know something about these brothers, of course, so we can imagine that this report was true, not fabricated. There is nothing in the text that leads us to conclude that Joseph consciously provoked his brothers with the "ill report." As we will see later in the chapter (Gen. 37:14), Jacob was in the habit of sending Joseph to check on his brothers. The boy may simply have been doing what his father requested. Joseph told the truth about his brothers, which, unfortunately, was not favorable to them. This undoubtedly provoked his brothers, but there is no reason to think it was conscious on Joseph's part.

2. a. Joseph's family assumed he was bragging about his superiority over them by the details of his dreams. They concluded that by dreaming this way, it was his intention to "have dominion" over them.

b. The other conclusion his family might have come to is actually hinted at in verse 11. Although Jacob rebuked him for the dream about "the sun, the moon, and the eleven stars" bowing down to Joseph, he did actually tuck the details of this dream away in his mind to think about. The family could have been *curious* about the meaning of the dreams, wondering if somehow Joseph had been marked out by God in some way for an unusual and unexpected future relationship with his father and brothers.

The Plot against Joseph (Gen. 37:12–28)

3. a. Responses will vary. Joseph was wearing the robe Jacob had made for him, which immediately stirred up the hostility his brothers felt towards him. Even from a distance, because of the robe, Joseph must have had a kind of royal bearing, which irritated the brothers. Because the brothers knew that Jacob often sent Joseph to check on them, perhaps they were up to no good when Joseph appeared (they were supposed to be in Shechem, not Dothan), which would have hardened their resentment against him. Their guilt, combined with their jealousy, turned to murderous wrath.

b. Responses will vary. The brothers were bitter over Joseph's elevated status among them, and they were determined that Joseph was not going to live a life of dominion over them. His dreams would turn out to be empty. In fact, his dreams would be completely reversed—instead of Joseph ruling over his brothers, they would rule over him, and finish him off.

c. Responses will vary. Reuben, Jacob's oldest son, wanted Joseph's life to be spared so he could "restore him to his father" (v. 22). It is hard to know whether this was prompted by concern for his brother or concern for his father. Reuben, remember, was the son who had slept with his father's concubine (see Gen. 35:22). That had been an act of rebellious disrespect for his father's authority. What effect did it have on Jacob (called "Israel" in the account)? We aren't told, but Reuben may have had remorse over it. When his brothers suggested killing Joseph, which Reuben knew would absolutely devastate Jacob, perhaps he was moved to compassion for father and son. Filial tenderness lay at the heart of Reuben's plan.

4. a. Responses will vary. The robe represented what the brothers hated about Joseph— their father's special favor on him. They vented their anger by removing the sign of his father's love, an act which must have expressed the thoughts of their hearts: "Your father cannot save you now."

b. Responses will vary. There isn't any record of what Joseph said or did while he was in the pit. Was he screaming for mercy? Did he ask questions about why they had done this to him? Did he cry uncontrollably? Was he silent out of fear?

Whatever was going on in the pit—either agonized yelling or agonized silence—Joseph's brothers were so unmoved by it that they were able to nonchalantly eat a meal and pay no attention to him.

c. Judah was reluctant to kill the boy, because he was their brother—"our own flesh." He didn't want Joseph to die, but he wanted him out of their lives. The appearance of the Ishmaelites made Judah realize that selling Joseph instead of killing him would not only remove him from them but would actually make some "profit" for them (v. 26). It was a much better plan, in every way.

"His Father Wept for Him" (Gen. 37:29–36)

5. a. Responses will vary. The brothers must have felt that Joseph's glorious robe was now useless. Did it give them cruel delight to smear it with blood and show it to their father, with their lie about Joseph's fate? Were they venting all their jealous resentment by desecrating the robe that way? For them, the bloody robe was proof that Joseph was no more—a problem solved. For Jacob, the sight of the bloody robe meant that the light had gone out of his life. A wound had opened that could never be healed.

b. Although his children "comforted" Jacob over the loss of Joseph, we know enough about them to be sure that their comfort was hollow. The agony their father suffered had been caused by their own hands! The words they offered to him couldn't possibly have come from love and devotion. They must have barely been able to conceal their joy that Joseph was finally gone. No wonder Jacob found no solace from them in his time of deep mourning.

Joseph in Egypt (Gen. 39:1–6a)

6. a. Potiphar recognized something in Joseph that his brothers had missed: he really *was* special, extraordinarily so. Although Potiphar, an Egyptian, did not know the God of the Hebrews, he could see from Joseph's competence and gifts that he was someone who had a divine ability to make everything he touched prosper. Joseph's dreams had not been his own delusions of grandeur. They had been signs of God's favor on him, which was clearly revealed in the work he did in Potiphar's house. Potiphar understood Joseph's true vocation: he was a blessed man and a source of blessing for others.

Joseph and Potiphar's Wife (Gen. 39:7–23)

7. a. Joseph refused to betray his master's confidence in him. Potiphar's wife wanted Joseph to take the one and only thing his master had not given him. Joseph refused to grasp at what was not his. To abuse his master's trust would have been a great wickedness, an offense against not just his master but against God Himself.

b. Responses will vary. Perhaps Joseph did not want to dishonor Potiphar's wife or his master by telling the true story. Perhaps his previous experience of having his garment stripped from him prepared him for the inevitability of another "death"—this time in prison, not a pit.

8. The Lord was with Joseph, even in prison. He was once again put in charge of everything, because the keeper of the prison could see that he was blessed and the source of blessing for everyone around him.

Pharaoh's Dreams (Gen. 41:14–45)

9. a. Joseph was a humble man who readily acknowledged that his unusual gifts came from God. In a golden moment, when he could have advanced his own cause by commending himself to Pharaoh, he willingly took the path of humility. Even the possibility of being free from prison and honored as the wisest man in the land did not tempt Joseph to forget God.

b. Responses will vary. We have to wonder whether Joseph's amazing elevation to the right hand of Pharaoh, with people bowing down before his chariot, made him think about his boyhood dreams of bowing sheaves and celestial bodies. Did the "garments of fine linen" in which he was arrayed remind him of the beautiful robe his father had made him? Was it a bittersweet experience for him to realize that much that he had lost when his brothers sold him had been regained—although not quite everything?

Joseph, Ruler in Egypt (Gen. 41:46–57)

10 a. Responses will vary. After his success in Pharaoh's court, Joseph was able, with God's help, to put behind him all his hardship and even memories of his father's house. His life was finally full and happy. He was not embittered by his many dreadful difficulties. He could even see God's hand of blessing in them all. Now that he had a family of his own, he could even let go of his longing for his father's house, which must have stayed with him for a very long time. By this point in his life, he had solid evidence that God loved him and was with him wherever he was, always blessing him and causing him to be a blessing to others. The land of his "affliction" had become the land of fruitfulness for him.

b. *Challenge question*: When Joseph was elevated to Pharaoh's right hand, it was not just Egypt that would benefit from his work and wisdom but "all the earth," because the famine was severe everywhere. God installed Joseph in a position that would allow him to provide bread (and life) even to his own family in Canaan. In Egypt, so many people had received blessing through Joseph. Now, would even his own brothers be counted among them?

Lesson 11

To make the most of this study, respond to all the questions yourself before reading these responses.

Famine in the Land of Canaan (Gen. 42:1–5)

1. a. Responses will vary. Jacob's fear about harm coming to Benjamin suggests to us that even though twenty years had passed since Joseph's disappearance, the wound in Jacob's heart had not fully healed. He had not forgotten that one day Joseph had gone out to look for his brothers and only his bloodied coat returned.

Jacob had perhaps settled all his love on Benjamin to make up for his loss. Even after so many years, Jacob must have lived daily with the fear that what had happened to Joseph could also happen to Benjamin. It was a thought he couldn't bear, so he kept his son at home when the brothers left for Egypt.

b. Responses will vary. Jacob apparently didn't trust his sons to take good care of Benjamin. We have to wonder whether he harbored lingering doubts about Joseph's mysterious disappearance twenty years before. Did the brothers resent Benjamin, as they had resented Joseph? Did Jacob think they were somehow responsible for Joseph's "death"? Had an undercurrent of suspicion run through this family ever since that episode?

Jacob's Sons Go Down to Egypt (Gen. 42:6–25)

2. a. *Challenge question*: Responses will vary. When Joseph saw his brothers bowing before him, just as they had done in his youthful dreams, he must have understood immediately that somehow God's plan for his life still included his family and that his long sojourn in Egypt had been a part of that plan. His brothers' cruel treatment of him had not thwarted the future that God had revealed to him in his dreams. The dreams had been true! This must have hit Joseph like a thunderbolt. Recall the names that Joseph had given his sons when they were born: "God has made me forget all my hardship and all my father's house," and "God has made me fruitful in the land of my affliction" (Gen. 41:50–52). Joseph had recognized God's goodness to him in Egypt, but he thought that the second part of his life had nothing to do with the first. He had, at last, been able to "forget" all his dreams and his family. Suddenly, when he saw his brothers bowing before him, he must have recognized that even his exile in slavery had been known by God all along. His family was not lost to him after all.

b. Responses will vary. Joseph was a man of great power in Egypt. If he had hated his brothers for what they did to him, he could have instantly revealed his identity and done away with them. He could have mocked them as they bowed low before him, reminding them that this was precisely the position they vowed they would never be in. If anger and revenge had filled Joseph's heart, this moment would have given him unlimited opportunities to vent it.

c. *Challenge question*: Joseph knew these men were his brothers, but he knew little else about them. He must have noticed right away that Benjamin was missing from among them. Joseph was probably curious about that. After they had sold him as a slave, had his brothers also harmed Benjamin, who would have taken his place as his father's favorite? Had they changed at all over the years?

Joseph accused his brothers of being spies, enemies who were seeking a way to harm Egypt, because he wanted to test them, know more about them. He wanted to see how much they would reveal about themselves as they rejected the accusation he made against them.

3. a. While they were in prison, the brothers experienced conviction of guilt over their shameful treatment of Joseph so long ago. Perhaps the confinement of the prison reminded them of their helpless young brother in the pit where they had thrown him. Why were they able to so quickly connect this terrible fate that had befallen them with a wrongdoing that had been hidden for twenty years? The only explanation is that they all suffered from guilty consciences. As they wondered about why something so terrible had happened to them—an unexpected and unjust imprisonment—they immediately remembered how unjust they had been to Joseph. The dishonest explanation of Joseph's disappearance they gave their father had not removed their guilt. It lay just beneath the surface of their lives. When they were helpless and in great fear, they could be honest about their offense. Reuben was convinced that this imprisonment was a just punishment for what they had done to Joseph.

b. Responses will vary. Joseph was overcome with emotion as he listened to his brothers' honesty and regret over their sin. No matter who his brothers had been when they first arrived in Egypt, these men, at long last, were finally honest sons of Jacob.

c. Responses will vary. Joseph wanted his brothers to fear him, to be fully aware of his power over them, for life or death. However, behind the appearance of his severity and wrath was his great love for his brothers. He charged them nothing for the grain they bought. It was his gracious gift to them, although they didn't know it. In their eyes, he was a harsh ruler who made a nearly impossible demand of them. They had no idea that love lay behind their great misfortune.

The Brothers Return to Egypt (Gen. 43:11–15)

4. a. In his first response to the need for Benjamin to go to Egypt, Jacob was consumed with his fears for his son and his lingering grief over Joseph. He could think only of his losses, and that made him hang on more tightly to what he had.

In his second response, Jacob was completely surrendered to God, asking for His mercy (v. 14) and willing to accept any suffering that might come to him: "If I am bereaved of my children, I am bereaved." He energetically directed the preparations for the trip, just as he had once energetically wrestled with an angel, refusing to let go until he received a blessing, even though his hip was out of joint. In this response, he was truly "Israel," trusting God beyond appearances.

b. *Challenge question:* Responses will vary. There were probably several factors that worked together to move Jacob from his first response to his second. The severity of the famine, of course, raised the stakes for his refusal to allow Benjamin to go to Egypt. If he persisted, all his sons would die. When the famine continued unabated, the prospect of great suffering gave Jacob an opportunity to think about times in his life when God had delivered him—from the wrath of Esau, from the treachery of Laban, from the spite of his brothers-in-law. God had faithfully kept all his promises to Jacob. Surely this was yet another occasion to put his trust in Him.

If Jacob had lingering doubts about his sons, the willingness of Reuben and Judah to make good on their promise to protect Benjamin (a resolve probably formed during their imprisonment in Egypt) must have convinced him that they could be trusted. No matter what had happened between Joseph and his brothers, this time the youngest among them would be safe. Jacob was then ready to let him go.

A Meal with Joseph (Gen. 43:16–25)

5. a. The brothers were fearful; they thought they would be punished for the money that had been returned to their sacks. They went straight to the steward and explained all that had happened. They offered to replace what they thought was missing money. The steward told them he had received their money. The only explanation for the treasure in their sacks was the goodness and favor of God.

b. Responses will vary. Joseph wanted desperately to be near Benjamin. He also wanted to make further inquiries about his father's well-being, which he could do more naturally in a dinner setting. So, in order to have communion with his brothers while he was still disguised from them, he threw a feast in his home and invited them to join him.

A Time to Make Merry (Gen. 43:26–34)

6. a. The brothers simply "drank and made merry" with Joseph without any apparent resentment or jealousy of Benjamin.

b. Responses will vary. This was a very happy scene, one that moved Joseph deeply. He witnessed for himself that his brothers did not begrudge the youngest the special favors he received. The only explanation for why Joseph did not reveal his identity is that there must have been something more he wanted to know about the men his brothers had become.

Judah and Joseph (Gen. 44:18–45:3)

7. a. Judah could not bear to break his father's heart and send him to his grave with grief. He was willing to do whatever was necessary to preserve his father's happiness, which was so bound up in Benjamin. Love for his father led him to lay down his life for his brother.

b. *Challenge question*: Responses will vary. When Joseph saw that Judah, the brother who had been responsible for his own exile in Egypt, was willing to lay down his life for Benjamin in order to save his father's joy, he knew everything he needed to know. His elaborate scheme of testing his brothers resulted in a purification of familial love. The brothers stood in solidarity with Benjamin, even when Joseph showered him with favor. Judah was willing to sacrifice himself for Benjamin, out of devotion to his father. The brothers' "three days" of imprisonment bore the fruit of true conversion in these men. Although they had sinned greatly against Joseph, their greatest sin had been against their father. Their worst failure had come in their disregard for what the loss of Joseph would mean to him.

As Judah spoke to him, Joseph perhaps realized that his boyhood dreams had been dramatically fulfilled. In them, he had seen both his brothers and his parents bowing down to him. When he had described them to his family in his youth, they had misunderstood. They thought he was making a claim of dominion over them. They couldn't have imagined that the bowing would one day represent their gratitude to him, not just because of the food he would be able to give them but because of the healing he would accomplish in their family life. Jacob's sons were finally true sons of their father, thanks to Joseph's rough talk, threats, and imprisonments.

The time for Joseph to reveal his identity had arrived.

A Joyful Reunion (Gen. 45:4–15)

8. a. Joseph didn't want his brothers to be angry with themselves for what they had done to him, because God had a purpose in all that had happened.

b. Joseph was able to forgive his brothers because he could see so clearly that although his brothers intended to do evil to him, God transformed it into good, for their family and for the whole world. Joseph had no bitterness over what had happened. Instead, he was full of joy to be reunited with his brothers. His love for them was stronger than the evil they had done against him.

c. Joseph wanted the family to be reunited. He wanted his father to come to him in Egypt. He wanted all the descendants of Jacob to dwell in safety, where there was plenty of food during the remainder of the famine. He wanted his family to be fully restored to him.

d. Joseph "kissed all his brothers and wept upon them." The brothers finally recovered from their shock and were able, at long last, to talk with him. The reunion and restoration of Jacob's family was finally underway.

Lesson 12

To make the most of this study, respond to all the questions yourself before reading these responses.

Israel Sets Out for Egypt (Gen. 46:1–7)

1. a. God made many wonderful promises to Jacob the first time he left the land of Canaan: (1) He promised to give to Jacob and his descendants the land on which he slept. (2) He promised to make Jacob's descendants too numerous to count. (3) He promised to make Jacob and his descendants a source of universal blessing. (4) He promised to go with him wherever he went, to "keep" him, and to bring him back to the land he had to leave.

b. In this second night vision, God promised many descendants ("a great nation") to Jacob, as He had done earlier. He also promised again to be with Jacob, this time in Egypt, and to return him to Canaan, just as He had done before.

c. *Challenge question*: Responses will vary. When Jacob left Canaan the first time, he did not offer any sacrifices to God; on his second departure, he did. That picture, recorded in Genesis 46:1, tells the whole story of what happened in between Jacob's two encounters with God.

Recall that in response to God's first appearance to him, Jacob vowed to make the God of his fathers his own God: "the LORD shall be my God" (Gen. 28:21). Through all his difficulties—trouble with his wives, trouble with his sons, fear of Esau, great suffering over the loss of Rachel and Joseph—Jacob learned to keep his promise to God. Look at the tenderness in this exchange between Jacob and God that did not appear in the first one. God spoke to him by name: "Jacob, Jacob." The answer was meek and humble: "Here am I." God calmed his fears about going to Egypt, and then He added a most amazing promise: "Joseph's hand shall close your eyes" (v.4) in death. Could there possibly have been any sweeter words to be uttered to Jacob than these? The face of the beloved son, whom Jacob had mourned all these years, would be the last earthly vision Jacob would have. This incredibly intimate exchange between God and Jacob proved that God's desire and Jacob's promise—that the Lord should be Jacob's God—had been richly fulfilled. The personal love between them is heartbreakingly beautiful.

Jacob's Family Settles in Goshen (Gen. 47:1–12)

2. a. Responses will vary. As Jacob was presented to Pharaoh, perhaps the promise of God to make him and his descendants a source of universal blessing was running through his head. When God had first made that promise to him, it probably sounded beyond impossible. How could a family of shepherds, living in the backwater of Canaan, ever even see other nations, let alone bless them? Could Jacob ever have imagined that he would one day be standing before the ruler of the greatest civilization on earth at that time? When it actually came to pass, Jacob must have recognized it as something only God could have made happen. He understood that now was his moment to exercise the priestly job God had given to Abraham and his descendants: Jacob blessed Pharaoh.

b. *Challenge question*: Responses will vary. When Jacob described his days as "few and evil," perhaps he was thinking about how many failures and shortcomings he had experienced in his life. He had cheated and lied to get his father's blessing; he had to flee his brother's wrath, never to see his mother again. His sons had caused him much heartache, and now he had left the land of promise. If the Egyptians were impressed by Jacob's age, it was only because they hadn't known Abraham and Isaac. In Jacob's mind, the passing generations of God's covenant family somehow had not lived up to their promising start. Already, in his day, the "golden age" of the great patriarchs was beginning to dim. He had no sense of his own greatness. He was humble and self–effacing—yet another fruit of his long life with God.

Jacob Prepares to Die (Gen. 47:27–31)

3. a. Responses will vary. We don't know for sure why Jacob's family remained in Egypt long after the famine ended. Surely the prosperity they experienced there had something to do with it. In Canaan, they had lived the semi-nomadic life of shepherds; in Goshen, they were settled in rich, fertile land. As their numbers increased, a sedentary life would have had great appeal. There was no need to keep on the move, loading and unloading their expanding families and possessions.

In addition, the culture of Egypt was highly advanced over the primitive culture of the Canaanites. Jacob's family certainly learned many skills and arts that they would never have known in their own country. As children were born and grew up in Egypt, that land became "home." As the years passed, so did any urgency to return to Canaan. Life was good in Egypt; why leave for a memory?

b. Jacob had a lively understanding of the importance of the land to Abraham's descendants. Within their future, promised by God, lay nationhood. Tribes of people cannot be a nation without land. Indeed, when Abraham arrived in the land of Canaan, from Haran, the first promise God made to him was to give him the land (Gen. 12:7), a promise that prompted Abraham to build the first altar to God there.

When God appeared to Jacob for the first time, Jacob awoke from his dream with a deep reverence for the land upon which he had slept: "Surely the Lord is in this place; and I did not know it. . . . How awesome is this place! This is none other than the house of God, and this is the gate of heaven" (Gen. 28:16–17). Jacob marked the holiness of that spot by building a pillar and anointing it with oil. He understood that the ground was holy because it was where the "ladder" from heaven touched down; the land was the sacred connection between heaven and earth.

As Jacob approached death, he remembered the great heritage he and his descendants had received from God in the gift of the land of Canaan. This was where they would be God's nation, to be a blessing to the whole world. There was simply no other place on earth like it; he must be buried there.

Jacob and Joseph's Sons (Gen. 48:1–32)

4. a. Jacob's heart was filled with awe and gratitude that he should see not only his beloved Joseph again but Joseph's sons as well. He seemed overwhelmed by the goodness of God. His terrible fears had been phantoms: he had received all his sons back, and more besides. At the end of his life, he was able to see how God had led him "all my life long to this day" (v. 15). He understood that his life had not been a random succession of calamities, although it must have felt that way from time to time. God had delivered him "from all evil" (v. 15). Confident faith replaced fear. Jacob knew from experience that "no eye has seen, nor ear heard, nor the heart of man conceived, what God has prepared for those who love him" (1 Cor. 2:9).

b. *Challenge question*: The irony in this scene is that Jacob had also been a younger son who received the blessing expected on the firstborn. Isaac's poor eyesight had made it possible for him to be tricked into doing what Rebekah and Jacob feared he wouldn't—give his blessing to Jacob, not Esau. Jacob, even with his bad eyesight, knew where his blessing belonged, although Joseph tried to change it. He did for himself what he hadn't given his own father a chance to do for himself: pass on the blessing of God to the right son.

c. Jacob assured Joseph that God would be with him and would return him to the land of Canaan. He gave to his son his own love and reverence for the land of God's promise.

d. Responses will vary. Perhaps because Joseph had been gone so long from the land of Canaan, Jacob thought he would not have a natural attachment to it. He had only been seventeen when he left; the bulk of his life had been spent in Egypt, living like an Egyptian. Jacob may have wanted to give Joseph a special stake in the land itself, to increase his interest in it and to make a return there seem more desirable. The gift may have been Jacob's way of making up to his son the life in Canaan he lost when his brothers sold him into slavery.

Jacob Breathed His Last (Gen. 49:28–50:3)

5. a. Jacob wanted to be buried with his people, with his fathers and his wife, Leah. It was not enough simply to be buried in the land of Canaan; he specifically desired to be buried in the same cave that held the bodies of those he loved.

b. Responses will vary. Perhaps in the seventeen years that Jacob had lived in Egypt and had watched his family settle in, he wondered whether they would lose their identity as descendants of Abraham, in a covenant with God. He may have thought that seeing the graves of their ancestors would keep alive their Hebrew identity and keep them conscious of the fact that Egypt was not their home.

Joseph and His Brothers (Gen. 50:15–21)

6. a. Responses will vary. Perhaps Joseph's brothers understood that the focus in his relationship with them had always been their father. He wanted them to be good sons to Jacob; he desired harmony in the family because it honored and pleased their father. Now that he was gone, they feared that there would be nothing to restrain whatever lingering anger Joseph may have felt toward them for their sins against him and Jacob. They used the memory of their father to invoke his continued favor upon them.

b. The brothers apologized for their transgression against Joseph; they asked for his forgiveness.

c. Responses will vary. It is hard to know what moved Joseph to tears in this scene. Did it hurt him to know that his brothers still anguished over their sin against him? That had always been a deep concern to him. Remember that when he finally revealed his identity to them, one of the very first things he said to them was, "[D]o not be distressed or angry with yourselves, because you sold me here" (Gen. 45:5). Did it grieve him to think he somehow hadn't adequately communicated his forgiveness to them? Were the tears from joy, because he could see how thoroughly and completely his brothers repented of what they had done? When they called themselves "the servants of the God of your father" (v. 17), was the poignant reminder of Jacob's faithful life with God too overwhelming for him?

Perhaps it was a touch of all these things that made Joseph weep before his brothers that day.

d. Joseph had already assured them that God had turned their evil into good (Gen. 45:5–8). He held no grudges against them. Since he could forgive them, they should be able to forgive themselves. Not only did he forgiven them, but he also intended to provide for them and their children. He had no intention of making them his servants. "Thus he reassured them and comforted them" (v. 21).

Joseph Dies (Gen. 50:22–26)

7. a. *Challenge question*: The definition of faith in Hebrews 11:1–2 is a perfect definition of the faith Saint Paul described in the patriarchs. They were men who lived with a conviction of what they couldn't "see"—the presence, power, and goodness of God, no matter what the circumstances. They all looked ahead, beyond appearances. Abraham offered Isaac with the hope of resurrection. Isaac, Jacob, and Joseph looked ahead to a future of national and worldwide blessing in and through their descendants, even though they were small in number and unsteady in virtue. They help us to see how much our lives with God require us to simply believe His word, His promises, His character.

b. *Challenge question*: The longing of a Christian's heart at death is to see God, to go home to heaven to be with Him there. Jacob and Joseph longed for the land of Canaan, because it was the holy connecting place of heaven and earth. In Christ, the union of heaven and earth takes place in human flesh, not land. If we are in Christ, we are fully reconciled with God in His family, the Church. All that is left is to behold His face, and death is the door that takes us home. As Saint Ignatius of Antioch said, "My earthly desire has been crucified; . . . there is living water in me, water that murmurs and says within me: Come to the Father [*Ad Rom.*, 6, 1–2, in *Apostolic Fathers*, II/2, 23–24]" (*Catechism*, no. 1011).

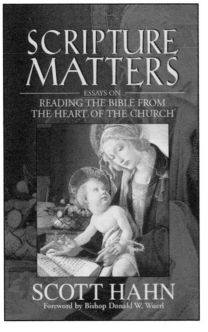

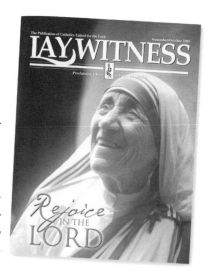